CANADIAN CONCEPTS

Second Edition

CONTENTS

UNIT	TOPICS
Getting Started Page 2	
1 **What's Your Name?** Page 9	The alphabet Names and titles
2 **Nice to Meet You** Page 21	Introductions Greetings
3 **How Many?** Page 35	Numbers The classroom Telephone numbers
4 **What's the Date?** Page 49	Days of the week Months of the year Ordinal numbers Birthdays Ages

GRAMMAR	LISTENING ACTIVITIES
Subject pronouns Verb "be"	Listening Activity 1: Nice to Meet You
Verb "be" contractions	Listening Activity 2: Names and Phone Numbers
Verb "be" questions	Listening Activity 3: Sorry, Wrong Number

UNIT		TOPICS
5	**Where Are You From?** Page 63	Countries Jobs Telephone conversations
6	**What Time Is It?** Page 77	Telling time Time zones Around the city
7	**Where Do You Live?** Page 97	Addresses Provinces of Canada Postal codes
8	**How Much Is It?** Page 109	Canadian money Food
9	**My Family** Page 125	Family members Physical descriptions
10	**How's the Weather?** Page 141	The weather Temperature The seasons Clothing Feelings Travel

GRAMMAR	LISTENING ACTIVITIES
Verb "be" negative	Listening Activity 4: Where Are You From? Listening Activity 5: What Do You Do?
Possessive nouns	Listening Activity 6: Is That A New Watch? Listening Activity 7: I'm Late
	Listening Activity 8: Name and Address
	Listening Activity 9: How Much Is It?
Verb "have"	Listening Activity 10: Who's in the Family?
	Listening Activity 11: Buying Clothes

TO THE TEACHER

The *Canadian Concepts* Series

The new edition of the popular *Canadian Concepts* series retains the Canadian focus designed to help students feel at home and integrate into the community. In the new edition, exercises and activities have been graded and, in some cases, refocussed to provide a careful build-up of skills throughout the series. *Canadian Concepts 1* is paced to accommodate the needs of post-literacy students, while *Canadian Concepts 2* moves ahead to introduce new vocabulary and grammatical structures at a faster pace. *Canadian Concepts 3* provides a richer field of vocabulary and a greater degree of challenge while reinforcing the themes of the lower levels. *Canadian Concepts 4, 5*, and *6* integrate video materials on Canadian themes.

The *Canadian Concepts* series uses a communicative approach. The method offers productive strategies for language learning based on student-centred interaction. Many new activities, games, and opportunities for speaking have been incorporated into the series to encourage maximum student participation in classroom activities. The pedagogical model presents students with challenging listening or reading input, leading them through pre-activities and strategies that make the input comprehensible. In addition to these fluency-building activities, dictation, grammar, spelling, and vocabulary work focus on improving students' accuracy.

Canadian Concepts 1

Canadian Concepts 1 provides ample practice with basic functional language. It is intended for students at the post-literacy stage. Students are encouraged to practise survival English phrases in meaningful contexts. A cast of characters appears throughout the book to engage students' interest, and language is carefully graded to help students become more proficient and confident as they move through the text.

Canadian Concepts 1 is made up of ten self-contained thematic units on survival English topics. Core activities focus on short, simple dialogues and reading texts that are designed to provide students with the language they need for their daily lives. Follow-up activities recycle language and concepts and lead the students into meaningful practice contexts.

Listening, speaking, reading, writing, grammar, pronunciation, and vocabulary-development exercises are integrated into all units. Clear illustrations and a picture dictionary at the bottom of each page lend valuable visual support for beginner students. A visual vocabulary review activity concludes each unit.

Teachers and students will appreciate the lively appearance and simple format of the materials. They will also enjoy browsing through "Canadian Capsules" that provide background information on Canada. The audio cassette tape has been recorded with concern for natural Canadian speech patterns. Worksheets to accompany many of the activities in *Canadian Concepts 1* are provided in the Teacher's Manual, with permission to photocopy.

KEY TO SYMBOLS

  Listening activity

  Reading activity

  Writing activity

  Work with a partner

  Work in a group

Teacher's Manual

A comprehensive Teacher's Manual provides step-by-step instructions keyed to the student book, answer keys, tape scripts, and teaching notes. Teaching tips and suggestions for optional activities for use in multi-level classrooms are incorporated.

Detailed teacher's notes are included to clarify the intention of activities and to make suggestions for promoting interaction in the classroom. These ideas will be appreciated by new teachers, while experienced teachers will find that the materials lend themselves to flexible interpretation and accommodate individual teaching styles.

At the End of the Course

Students who successfully complete this level will be ready for *Canadian Concepts 2*, a book for false beginners. *Canadian Concepts 2* builds on the post-literacy survival English base of *Canadian Concepts 1* and moves ahead at a more challenging pace.

CANADIAN CONCEPTS

Second Edition

GETTING STARTED

Classroom Instructions

1. Open your book at page 6.

2. Look at the pictures.

3. Practise with the teacher.

4. Say the word.

5. Read the story.

6. Listen.

7. Talk to your partner.

8. Please spell it.

9. Turn the page.

10. Write the answers.

11. Repeat.

12. Copy.

13. A chart.

14. Answer the questions.

15. Complete.

16. Choose the answer.

The Classroom

a ceiling

a light

a map

a clock

a window

a wall

a door

an eraser

a board

a piece of chalk

a desk

a floor

a globe

an apple

a pencil

a desk

a cup

a book

a pen

a chair

a chair

a wastepaper basket

The World

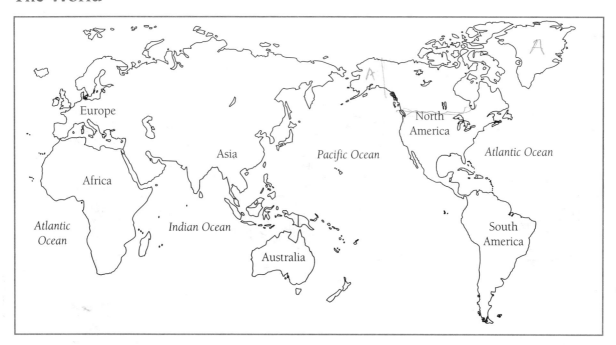

Canada

Letters of the Alphabet

Print

Aa Bb Cc Dd Ee Ff Gg Hh Ii Jj Kk Ll Mm Nn Oo Pp Qq Rr Ss Tt Uu Vv Ww Xx Yy Zz

Write

Aa Bb Cc Dd Ee Ff Gg Hh Ii Jj Kk Ll Mm Nn Oo Pp Qq Rr Ss Tt Uu Vv Ww Xx Yy Zz

Cardinal Numbers

1	one	26	twenty-six	51	fifty-one	76	seventy-six
2	two	27	twenty-seven	52	fifty-two	77	seventy-seven
3	three	28	twenty-eight	53	fifty-three	78	seventy-eight
4	four	29	twenty-nine	54	fifty-four	79	seventy-nine
5	five	30	thirty	55	fifty-five	80	eighty
6	six	31	thirty-one	56	fifty-six	81	eighty-one
7	seven	32	thirty-two	57	fifty-seven	82	eighty-two
8	eight	33	thirty-three	58	fifty-eight	83	eighty-three
9	nine	34	thirty-four	59	fifty-nine	84	eighty-four
10	ten	35	thirty-five	60	sixty	85	eighty-five
11	eleven	36	thirty-six	61	sixty-one	86	eighty-six
12	twelve	37	thirty-seven	62	sixty-two	87	eighty-seven
13	thirteen	38	thirty-eight	63	sixty-three	88	eighty-eight
14	fourteen	39	thirty-nine	64	sixty-four	89	eighty-nine
15	fifteen	40	forty	65	sixty-five	90	ninety
16	sixteen	41	forty-one	66	sixty-six	91	ninety-one
17	seventeen	42	forty-two	67	sixty seven	92	ninety-two
18	eighteen	43	forty-three	68	sixty-eight	93	ninety-three
19	nineteen	44	forty-four	69	sixty-nine	94	ninety-four
20	twenty	45	forty-five	70	seventy	95	ninety-five
21	twenty-one	46	forty-six	71	seventy-one	96	ninety-six
22	twenty-two	47	forty-seven	72	seventy-two	97	ninety-seven
23	twenty-three	48	forty-eight	73	seventy-three	98	ninety-eight
24	twenty-four	49	forty-nine	74	seventy-four	99	ninety-nine
25	twenty-five	50	fifty	75	seventy-five	100	one hundred

Ordinal Numbers

1st first	11th eleventh	21st twenty-first
2nd second	12th twelfth	22nd twenty-second
3rd third	13th thirteenth	23rd twenty-third
4th fourth	14th fourteenth	24th twenty-fourth
5th fifth	15th fifteenth	25th twenty-fifth
6th sixth	16th sixteenth	26th twenty-sixth
7th seventh	17th seventeenth	27th twenty-seventh
8th eighth	18th eighteenth	28th twenty-eighth
9th ninth	19th nineteenth	39th twenty-ninth
10th tenth	20th twentieth	30th thirtieth
		31st thirty-first

Days of the Week

Monday	(Mon.)
Tuesday	(Tues.)
Wednesday	(Wed.)
Thursday	(Thurs.)
Friday	(Fri.)
Saturday	(Sat.)
Sunday	(Sun.)

Months of the Year

January	(Jan.)
February	(Feb.)
March	(Mar.)
April	(Apr.)
May	
June	
July	
August	(Aug.)
September	(Sept.)
October	(Oct.)
November	(Nov.)
December	(Dec.)

Shapes

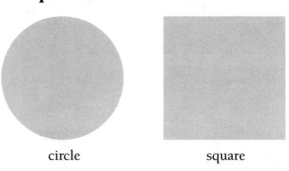

circle   square

rectangle

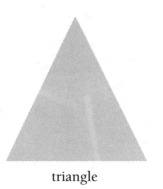

triangle

UNIT 1

WHAT'S YOUR NAME?

CAPITAL LETTERS

A Practise the letters of the alphabet with the teacher.

A B C D E F G H I J K L M N O P Q R S T U V W X Y Z

A B C D E F G H I J K L M N O P Q R S T U V W X Y Z

B Match the letters. Use the worksheet.

A	*E*	J	*L*	S	*V*
B	*G*	K	*M*	T	*Y*
C	*I*	L	*O*	U	*W*
D	*A*	M	*J*	V	*S*
E	*H*	N	*Q*	W	*Z*
F	*B*	O	*K*	X	*T*
G	*C*	P	*N*	Y	*X*
H	*F*	Q	*R*	Z	*U*
I	*D*	R	*P*		

9

C Write the letters. Use the worksheet.

1. a _B_ C D _E_ F g _H_ _I_ _J_ K L
2. g _H_ _I_ K L M _N_ O _P_ Q R
3. K L _M_ N _O_ P Q R _S_ T U V
4. O _P_ Q R T J U V _W_ X Y Z
5. D _E_ F _I_ _H_ L M K L M N O

SMALL LETTERS

A Practise the letters with the teacher.

a b c d e f g h i j k l m n o p q r s t u v w x y z

a b c d e f g h i j k l m n o p q r s t u v w x y z

B Match the letters. Use the worksheet.

a	*e*	j	*l*	s	*u*
b	*g*	k	*n*	t	*y*
c	*b*	l	*j*	u	*z*
d	*f*	m	*r*	v	*x*
e	*a*	n	*q*	w	*s*
f	*i*	o	*k*	x	*v*
g	*h*	p	*m*	y	*w*
h	*c*	q	*p*	z	*t*
i	*d*	r	*o*		

C Write the letters. Use the worksheet.

1. a b c _d_ e f g _h_ i _j_ k _l_
2. d _e_ f g h _i_ j e l _m_ n o

a capital letter   a small letter   to repeat   to match   a worksheet

3. g h *j i k l* m n o p g r

4. l *m* n o p q r s t u *v* w

5. n o *p q* o s t y *v* w *x* y z

D Listen to the teacher. Circle the letter you hear. Use the worksheet.

1. l r	7. m n	13. x z
2. e i	8. u w	14. t v
3. b e	9. j g	15. h k
4. v w	10. a e	16. g b
5. k q	11. c d	17. f v
6. p t	12. h y	18. l e

NAMES

A Listen to the teacher. Write the first names. Use your notebook.

B Match the family names.

1.	JOHNSON	a) *Williams*
2.	WILLIAMS	b) *Rose*
3.	WILSON	c) *Clark*
4.	CLARK	d) *Majors*
5.	CLINTON	e) *Masters*
6.	ROSS	f) *Clinton*
7.	ROSE	g) *Johnson*
8.	MAJORS	h) *Ross*
9.	MASTERS	i) *Wilson*

to write   a teacher   a first name   a family name   a notebook

C   Complete the names from Exercise B.

1. M a _r_ o _s_ s
2. R _o_ s s
3. C l _a_ _r_ k
4. _W_ i l _s_ o n
5. R _o_ s _a_
6. _C_ l i n _t_ o n
7. M _a_ s _ e r _
8. J _o_ h _n_ _s_ o _n_
9. W _i_ l _l_ _i_ a m s

WHAT IS YOUR NAME?

A   Look.

Kate Martin

What is your name?

First name	Family name
Kate	

What is your family name?

First name	Family name
	Martin

CANADIAN CAPSULES   In Canada, "Smith" is the most common English name and "Tremblay" is the most common French name.

to look

to circle   to hear   to listen   to complete

What is your name?

First name	Family name	
Jun		

Jun Kim

What is your last name?

First name	Last name	
	Kim	

a book   paper   a pen   a pencil   an eraser

B   Write.

What is your name? Use your notebook.

First name	Family name	

C   Practise with the teacher.

Conversation 1

Jun: Hi, what is your name?

Kate: My name is Kate.

Jun: What is your last name?

Kate: My last name is Martin.

Conversation 2

Kate: Hi, what is your name?

Jun: My name is Jun.

Kate: What is your family name?

Jun: My family name is Kim.

    D   Talk with a partner. Ask and answer the questions.

> Hi, what is your name?
>
> My name is _____.
>
> What is your family/last name?
>
> My last name is _____.

to practise   to talk   a partner   to ask   to answer

E Complete the forms together. Use the worksheet.

1. My name is

First name   Last name

2. My partner is

First name   Last name

WHO ARE THEY?

A Listen to the teacher. Write the names of students in the class. Use your notebook.

GREETINGS AND TITLES

Mr.   Ms.   Miss   Mrs.   Dr.

a question   a form   a student   a class   a teacher

A   Look and practise with the teacher.

Mr. (Mister) Carlos Lopez
Say: Hi, Carlos.
        Hello, Mr. Lopez.

Ms. Kate Martin
Say: Hi, Kate.
        Hello, Ms. Martin.

Miss Mona Aziz
Say: Hi, Mona.
        Hello, Miss Aziz.

Mrs. (Missus) Olga Kuslov
Say: Hi, Olga.
        Hello, Mrs. Kuslov.

a doctor   a man   a woman   a family   to say

B   Look and practise with the teacher.

Right: ✔ Hi, Jun.   Wrong: ✘ Hello, Ms. Kate.
         ✔ Hello, Mr. Kim.   ✘ Hello, Mr. Carlos.

Right: ✔ Hi, Mona.   ✘ Hello, Mrs. Olga.
         ✔ Hello, Miss Aziz.   ✘ Hello, Miss Lili.

Right: ✔ Hi, Kate.   Wrong: ✘ Hello, teacher.
         ✔ Hello, Ms. Martin.   ✘ Hello, Mrs. teacher.

Right: ✔ Hi, Ana.   ✘ Hello, my teacher.
         ✔ Hello, Mrs. Lopez.

C   Choose greetings from page 18 for the people in the picture.

> a)   Hello, Ms. Kate.
> ✔ b)   Hello, Ms. Martin.

1. a) Hello, Mr. Michel Banon.
    b) Hello, Mr. Banon.

2. a) Hello, Jun.
    b) Hello, Mr. Jun.

3. a) Hello, Miss Lopez.
    b) Hello, Mrs. Lopez.

4. a) Hi, Mr. Max.
    b) Hi, Mr. Kuslov.

5. a) Hi, Mona.
    b) Hi, Miss Mona.

6. a) Hello, Olga.
    b) Hello, Mrs. Olga.

7. a) Hi, Mr. Lopez.
    b) Hi, Mr. Carlos.

8. a) Hello, Ms. Han.
    b) Hello, Ms. Lili.

D   Greet the person. Use a title.

> Kate: Hello, my name is Kate Martin.
> **Hello, Ms. Martin.**

1. Michel: Hello, my name is Michel Banon.

    Hello, _____.

2. Mona: Hello, my name is Mona Aziz.

    Hi,_____.

3. Jun: Hello, my name is Jun Kim.

    Hello, _____.

4. Max: Hello, my name is Max Kuslov.

    Hello, _____.

5. Olga: Hi, my name is Olga Kuslov.

    Hi, _____.

a title   a boy   a girl   a child   children

6. Lili: Hi, my name is Lili Han.

Hi, _____.

7. Ana: Hi, my name is Ana Lopez.

Hi, _____.

8. Carlos: Hello, my name is Carlos Lopez.

Hello, _____.

E Complete the forms for you and your partner. Use the worksheet.

(Ms.) Mrs. Miss Mr.

| H | A | N | | | | | | |

Last name

| L | I | L | I | | | | | |

First name

Ms. Mrs. Miss Mr.

| | | | | | | | | |

Last name

| | | | | | | | | |

First name

Ms. Mrs. Miss Mr.

| | | | | | | | | |

Last name

| | | | | | | | | |

First name

a person   people   a classroom   to read   to open

WORD REVIEW

Write the words for the pictures.

A 1	a 2	*Kate Martin* 3	*Kate Martin* 4
5	6	7	8
9	10	11	12
WELCOME! 13	SURVEY Mr. Miss Mrs. Ms. 14	We are students 15	16
17	18	19	20

a book
a capital letter
a child
a class
a classroom
a doctor
a family
a family name
a first name
a greeting
a partner
a pen
a pencil
a small letter
a student
a teacher
children
people
to circle
to complete

UNIT 2
NICE TO MEET YOU

THE ENGLISH CLASS

A Read with the teacher.

This is Mona Aziz. **She** is a woman.

This is Carlos Lopez. This is Ana Lopez. **They** are married.

This is Jun Kim. **He** is a man.

This is Olga Kuslov. This is Max Kuslov. **They** are married.

This is Michel Banon. **He** is a student in the class.

This is Lili Han. **She** is a woman.

  B Read the sentences with a partner.

21

GRAMMAR FOCUS   **Subject Pronouns**

A   Look.

B   Write the pronouns.

Jun   Ana   Max   Olga   cat

I am Kate.

1. _____ is Jun

2. _____ is Kate.

3. _____ are Max and Olga.

4. _____ is a cat.

friends   a conversation   married   single   a cat

C   Find the pronouns in the sentences. Write the pronouns in your notebook.

> This is Max. He is a student.   **he**

1. My name is Kate. I am a teacher.
2. This is Carlos. He is a man.
3. My friend is Mona. She is a woman.
4. These are my friends. They are married.
5. This is my friend. He is a student.
6. Meet Jun Kim. He is a man.
7. My friends are Lili and Ana. They are women.
8. This is my classroom. It is big.
9. Meet Max and Olga. They are married.
10. This is my cat. It is young.

D   Write the pronouns.

> Michel.   **he**

1. a man
2. students
3. a desk
4. Ana and Carlos
5. a pencil
6. a woman
7. a teacher
8. a book
9. my partner
10. Mona and Kate
11. a student
12. my partner and I
13. Jun and Michel
14. the class
15. Olga
16. the teacher and students
17. paper
18. a man and woman
19. my friend
20. a dog

a dog   big (fish)   small (fish)   young   old

NICE TO MEET YOU

LISTENING ACTIVITY 1

A Practise with the teacher.

> Nice to meet you.
>
> I'm pleased to meet you.

B Listen and complete the conversations. Use the worksheet.

Conversation 1

Lili: Hi. I'm Lili.

Ana: Hello, Lili. _____ to meet you. I'm Ana.

Lili: Hello, Ana. I'm _____ to meet you.

Conversation 2

Max: Hello. I'm Max.

Michel: Hi, Max. Nice to _____ you. My name is Michel.

Max: I'm _____ to meet you, Michel.

Conversation 3

Mona: Hello. My name is Mona.

Olga: Hi, Mona. I'm pleased to _____ you. My name is Olga.

Mona: _____ to meet you Olga.

C Walk around the classroom. Greet your classmates.

to walk   an apple   happy   pleased   sad

GIVING PERSONAL INFORMATION

A   Look.

male   **female**

single   married

divorced

CANADIAN CAPSULES   A nickname is a short or special form of a name. For example, the nickname for "William" is "Bill."

male   female   married   single   divorced

B   Write a title.

Person	Title	
Kate Martin 　single 　female	**Ms. Martin**	
Michel Banon 　single 　male		
Lili Han 　divorced 　female		
Max Kuslov 　married 　male		
Ana Lopez 　married 　female		
Mona Aziz 　single 　female		
Olga Kuslov 　married 　female		
Jun Kim 　single 　male		
Carlos Lopez 　married 　male		

a school　　a house　　an apartment building　　a street　　a city

C   Complete the forms. Use the worksheet.

Ms. (Mr.) Miss   Mrs.

Last name _____**Kim**_____   First name _____**Jun**_____

Sex: (male) female

Marital status: (single) married   divorced

Ms.   Mr.   Miss   Mrs.

Last name _____   First name _____**Max**_____

Sex: male   female

Marital status: single   married   divorced

Ms.   Mr.   Miss   Mrs.

Last name _____   First name _____**Ana**_____

Sex: male   female

Marital status: single   married   divorced

Ms.   Mr.   Miss   Mrs.

Last name _____**Aziz**_____   First name _____

Sex: male   female

Marital status: single   married   divorced

Ms.   Mr.   Miss   Mrs.

Last name _____   First name _____**Lili**_____

Sex: male   female

Marital status: single   married   divorced

Ms.   Mr.   Miss   Mrs.

Last name _____**Banon**_____   First name _____

Sex: male   female

Marital status: single   married   divorced

a car   a truck   a bus   a bus stop   a subway

Ms.   Mr.   Miss   Mrs.

Last name _____   First name _____**Olga**_____

Sex: male   female

Marital status: single   married   divorced

Ms.   Mr.   Miss   Mrs.

Last name _____**Lopez**_____   First name _____

Sex: male   female

Marital status: single   married   divorced

NEW FRIENDS

A   Look and practise with the teacher.

a man
a woman
a child
young/old
happy/sad

new

old

to open

to close

a door

B   Look at the picture.

   C   Read the sentences with a partner. Say "yes" or "no."

Carlos is a woman	**no**

1. Ana is happy.
2. Max and Olga are married.
3. Masha is young. She is a child.
4. Michel is happy.
5. Mario is old.
6. Lili is a child.
7. Ana is a man.
8. Olga is a woman.

9. Max is old.
10. Ana and Max are married.
11. Michel is a man.
12. Olga is old.
13. Carlos is happy.
14. Mario is young.
15. Ana and Mario are married.

a child   a baby   tall   short   tired

D Write two sentences about yourself. Use your notebook.

> **I am a woman. I am happy.**

I am: a man   a woman   a child

I am: happy   sad

GRAMMAR FOCUS

Verb "Be"

A Look.

Use **be** in sentences with no action.

I am
you **are**
he **is**
she **is**
it **is**
we **are**
you **are**
they **are**

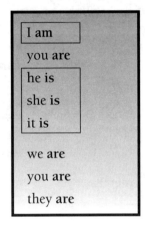

CANADIAN CAPSULES

In Canada, the average age at marriage is 25 for women and 27 for men.

near   far   strong   weak   hungry

B   Look at the pictures. Complete the sentences.

He is a man.

1   _____ students.   4   _____ married.

2   _____ a woman.   5   _____ single.

3   _____ a pencil.   6   _____ a book.

thirsty   sleepy   angry   early   late

C   Write the verb.

I **am** a student.

1.   She _____ a woman.

2.   My book _____ old.

3.   He _____ young.

4.   Max and Jun _____ men.

5.   Kate _____ a woman.

6.   Lili and Mona _____ happy.

7.   Michel _____ a young man.

8.   Ana _____ a young woman.

9.   He _____ Max Kuslov.

10. I _____ Michel Banon.

11. Jun and I _____ friends.

12. Mona and I _____ students.

13. Mario and Henri _____ old.

14. Masha _____ a child.

a job

to work

busy

worried

sick

WORD REVIEW

Write the words for the pictures.

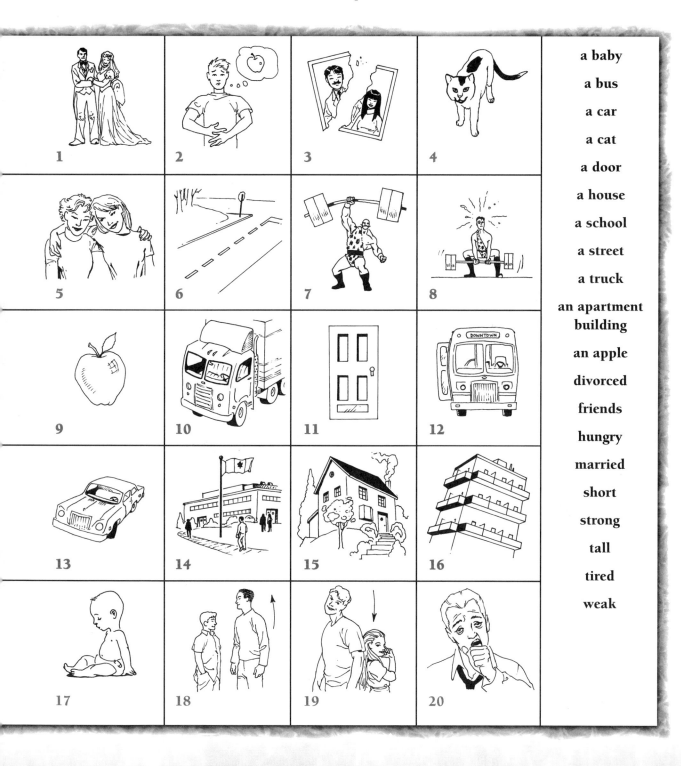

1	2	3	4	a baby
5	6	7	8	a bus
9	10	11	12	a car
13	14	15	16	a cat
17	18	19	20	a door

a baby
a bus
a car
a cat
a door
a house
a school
a street
a truck
an apartment building
an apple
divorced
friends
hungry
married
short
strong
tall
tired
weak

3

HOW MANY?

NUMBERS

A Say the numbers with the teacher.

1	2	3	4	5	6	7	8	9	10
11	12	13	14	15	16	17	18	19	20
21	22	23	24	25	26	27	28	29	30
31	32	33	34	35	36	37	38	39	40

B Read the numbers with the teacher.

one	thirteen	twenty-five	thirty-seven
two	fourteen	twenty-six	thirty-eight
three	fifteen	twenty-seven	thirty-nine
four	sixteen	twenty-eight	forty
five	seventeen	twenty-nine	. . . .
six	eighteen	thirty	fifty
seven	nineteen	thirty-one	sixty
eight	twenty	thirty-two	seventy
nine	twenty-one	thirty-three	eighty
ten	twenty-two	thirty-four	ninety
eleven	twenty-three	thirty-five	one hundred
twelve	twenty-four	thirty-six	

C　Match the words and numbers.

1.	twenty-one	a)	12
2.	thirty-three	b)	16
3.	fourteen	c)	9
4.	sixteen	d)	21
5.	nine	e)	17
6.	eleven	f)	22
7.	thirty	g)	33
8.	seventeen	h)	14
9.	twenty-two	i)	11
10.	twelve	j)	30

D　Write the numbers.

1. forty-six		14. forty-three
2. seven		15. seventeen
3. sixty-six		16. eighty-seven
4. one hundred		17. forty-nine
5. ten		18. eighteen
6. sixteen		19. five
7. thirty-nine		20. twelve
8. eighty-two		21. seventy
9. nine		22. thirty-four
10. twenty-two		23. eleven
11. eighteen		24. twenty-three
12. twenty-six		25. eighty
13. ninety-three		

forty-six

a word

46

a number

to read

to match

to write

E   Listen to the teacher. Circle the numbers you hear. Use the worksheet.

1.   a)   24   6.   a)   15
    b)   44   b)   12
    c)   42   c)   13

2.   a)   29   7.   a)   6
    b)   19   b)   26
    c)   9   c)   16

3.   a)   18   8.   a)   5
    b)   16   b)   15
    c)   26   c)   25

4.   a)   22   9.   a)   3
    b)   42   b)   33
    c)   14   c)   23

5.   a)   11   10.   a)   2
    b)   21   b)   12
    c)   12   c)   32

CANADIAN CAPSULES   The population of Canada is 28 million people.

to listen   full   empty   excited   nervous

COUNTING

How many asks about numbers.

How many days are in a week?   **seven**

How many apples are in each picture?
Write the number for each picture.

10

to count   a day   a week   an apple   a picture

IN THE CLASSROOM

A   Say the words with the teacher.

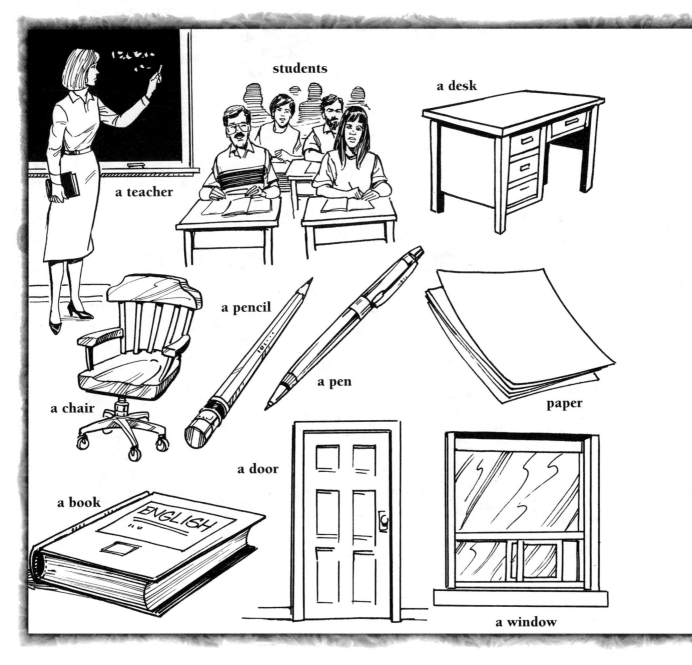

students

a desk

a teacher

a pencil

a pen

paper

a chair

a door

a book

ENGLISH

a window

a desk

a chair

a pencil

a pen

paper

B   Look at the picture. Answer the questions on page 41. Count and write the numbers. Use your notebook.

a book

a door

a window

to sit

to stand

1. How many teachers?
2. How many students?
3. How many males?
4. How many females?
5. How many books?

6. How many desks?
7. How many chairs?
8. How many windows?
9. How many doors?
10. How many pencils?

C Count the things in **your** classroom. Write the answers.

1. How many teachers?
2. How many students?
3. How many males?
4. How many females?
5. How many books?

6. How many desks?
7. How many chairs?
8. How many windows?
9. How many doors?
10. How many pencils?

TELEPHONE NUMBERS

A Listen to the teacher. Circle the telephone numbers you hear. Use the worksheet.

WHAT IS YOUR TELEPHONE NUMBER?

MY TELEPHONE NUMBER IS 731-9760

1. 681-1221   681-2112
2. 486-7895   488-7985
3. 325-0119   325-9011
4. 874-4356   485-4356
5. 293-7650   293-7500
6. 243-9078   342-9078
7. 318-4595   318-4955
8. 406-9012   406-1290

a male

a female

a telephone

a telephone number

a postal code

B   Listen to the teacher. Write the telephone numbers. Use your notebook.

C   Copy the chart in your notebook. Write the names or numbers in the chart.

Lili	282-1801
Carlos and Ana	336-4339
Mona	731-9760
Michel	270-4876
Max and Olga	736-2015
Jun	849-0548
Kate	875-4238

Name	Phone number
Lili	282-1801
Carlos and Ana	
	731-0760
Michel	
	736-2015
	849-0548
Kate	

CANADIAN CAPSULES   The numbers we use are called Arabic numbers. Sometimes we use Roman numerals, such as I, II, III, IV, V.

to copy

a chart

1, 2, 3, 4
Arabic numbers

I, II, III, IV
Roman numerals

Janet Simmons
a name

 **Verb "Be" Contractions**

Contractions join two words.

I am ⟶ I'm

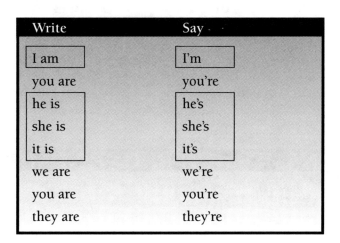

Write	Say
I am	I'm
you are	you're
he is	he's
she is	she's
it is	it's
we are	we're
you are	you're
they are	they're

A Write the contractions.

I am Michel.	**I'm Michel.**

1. She is a woman.
2. It is my desk.
3. They are my friends.
4. We are students.
5. He is a teacher.
6. They are male.
7. It is my number.
8. You are a student.
9. He is Max.
10. They are students.
11. She is my teacher.
12. We are friends.
13. I am a student.
14. You are my friend.
15. He is a man.

$$\frac{\begin{array}{r} 3 \\ +\,4 \end{array}}{7}\ \checkmark$$

right

$$\frac{\begin{array}{r} 3 \\ +\,4 \end{array}}{6}\ \times$$

wrong

$$\frac{\begin{array}{r} 2 \\ +\,3 \end{array}}{5}$$

easy

$$\frac{\begin{array}{r} 253\,389 \\ \times\,63\,820 \end{array}}{?}$$

hard

I'm

to join

B   Write the full form.

> He's Carlos Lopez.   **He is Carlos Lopez.**

1. They're students.
2. It's 533-6014.
3. He's a man.
4. We're women.
5. I'm in the classroom.

6. It's my pen.
7. She's my friend.
8. They're Max and Olga.
9. We're teachers.
10. I'm Kate Martin.

NAMES AND PHONE NUMBERS

LISTENING ACTIVITY 2

A   Practise with the teacher.

Conversation 1

Clerk: Good morning.

Max: Hello.

Clerk: What is your family name?

Max: Kuslov

Clerk: Please spell it.

Max: K U S L O V

Clerk: What is your first name?

Max: Max

Clerk: What is your phone number?

Max: It's 731-9760.

full form

contraction

"Good morning"

"Good evening"

"Good night"

Conversation 2

Clerk:	Good morning.
Lili:	Hello.
Clerk:	What is your last name?
Lili:	My last name?
Clerk:	Yes, what is your family name?
Lili:	Han
Clerk:	What is your first name?
Lili:	Lili, L I L I
Clerk:	What is your phone number?
Lili:	It's 523 -5664.

 B Practise the conversations with a partner.

 C Listen and write the words. Use the worksheet.

Conversation 1

Clerk:	Good morning.
Man:	Hello.
Clerk:	What is your last name?
Man:	_____
Clerk:	What is your first name?
Man:	_____
Clerk:	What is your phone number?
Man:	_____

a phone number

to spell

to say

a clerk

a telephone book

Conversation 2

Clerk: Good morning.

Woman: Hello.

Clerk: What is your family name?

Woman: _____

Clerk: What is your first name?

Woman: _____

Clerk: What is your telephone number?

Woman: _____

D   Ask three people. Write the answers in your notebook.

Good morning.

Hello.

What is your last name? Please spell it.

_____

What is your first name?

_____

What is your phone number?

_____

a receiver

a cord

a cellular
phone

a dial

buttons

WORD REVIEW

Write the words for the pictures.

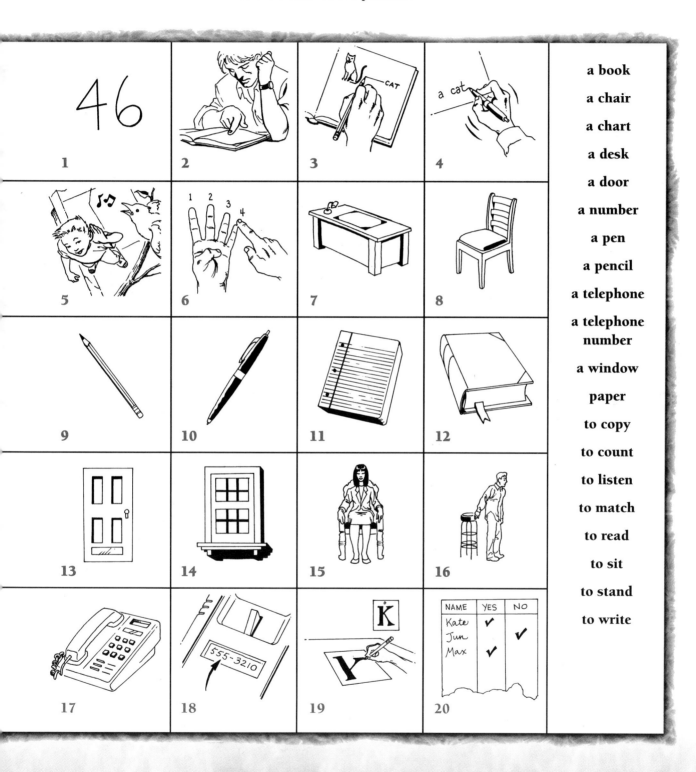

				a book
1	2	3	4	a chair
				a chart
				a desk
				a door
5	6	7	8	a number
				a pen
				a pencil
				a telephone
9	10	11	12	a telephone number
				a window
				paper
				to copy
13	14	15	16	to count
				to listen
				to match
				to read
17	18	19	20	to sit
				to stand
				to write

UNIT 4

WHAT'S THE DATE?

DAYS OF THE WEEK

A   Say the days with the teacher.

Sunday (Sun.)	Monday (Mon.)	Tuesday (Tues.)	Wednesday (Wed.)	Thursday (Thurs.)	Friday (Fri.)	Saturday (Sat.)
	1	2	3	4	5	6
7	8	9	10	11	12	13
14	15	16	17	18	19	20
21	22	23	24	25	26	27
28	29	30	31			

B   Listen to the teacher. Circle the word you hear. Use the worksheet.

1. a) Monday   4. a) Sunday
   b) Sunday   b) Tuesday
   c) Saturday   c) Thursday

2. a) Wednesday   5. a) Tuesday
   b) Tuesday   b) Thursday
   c) Thursday   c) Saturday

3. a) Friday   6. a) Thursday
   b) Saturday   b) Tuesday
   c) Thursday   c) Friday

C   Complete the words. Then match. Use the worksheet.

1. T u __ s d __ y   a) Mon.

2. M __ n __ __ y   b) Thurs.

3. S __ __ u r __ a __   c) Fri.

4. __ e __ n __ s __ __ y   d) Wed.

5. F __ i __ a __   e) Tues.

6. __ h __ r s __ __ y   f) Sun.

7. __ u __ d __ y   g) Sat.

CANADIAN CAPSULES   1867 is the year of Canadian Confederation. July 1 is Canada's birthday.

a calendar   a day   a week   a month   a year

MONTHS OF THE YEAR

A Say the months with the teacher.

January **(Jan.)**	**February** **(Feb.)**	**March** **(Mar.)**	**April** **(Apr.)**
May	**June**	**July**	**August** **(Aug.)**
September **(Sept.)**	**October** **(Oct.)**	**November** **(Nov.)**	**December** **(Dec.)**

B Listen to the teacher. Circle the month you hear. Use the worksheet.

1. a) January
   b) June

2. a) March
   b) May

3. a) May
   b) July

4. a) September
   b) November

5. a) August
   b) October

6. a) December
   b) November

7. a) February
   b) January

8. a) June
   b) April

9. a) March
   b) February

10. a) October
    b) February

January or **Jan.**
an abbreviation

turn left

turn right

top

bottom

C   Write the months. Use your notebook.

1. January _____ March _____ May
    _____ _____ August _____
    _____ November   December

2. _____ February _____ April
    _____ June _____ _____
    September _____ _____ December

THE CALENDAR

A   Complete the calendar. Use the worksheet.

J __ n __ a __ y						
S_nd__	Monda_	T_es_ay	W__nes_ay	T_ur_da_	F_i_a_	_atu_d_y
		1	2	3		5
	7	8		10	11	
13		15	16		18	19
20	21	22	23		25	26
	28	29	30	31		

to study

to do homework

to learn

to see

to rest

ORDINAL NUMBERS

Ordinal numbers put things in order

| 1, 2, 3...   first, second, third,... |

A Say the numbers with the teacher.

1st first	11th eleventh	21st twenty-first
2nd second	12th twelfth	22nd twenty-second
3rd third	13th thirteenth	23rd twenty-third
4th fourth	14th fourteenth	24th twenty-fourth
5th fifth	15th fifteenth	25th twenty-fifth
6th sixth	16th sixteenth	26th twenty-sixth
7th seventh	17th seventeenth	27th twenty-seventh
8th eighth	18th eighteenth	28th twenty-eighth
9th ninth	19th nineteenth	39th twenty-ninth
10th tenth	20th twentieth	30th thirtieth
		31st thirty-first

B Listen to the teacher. Circle the word you hear. Use the worksheet.

1. a) first
    b) twenty-first

2. a) ninth
    b) nineteenth

3. a) twelfth
    b) twentieth

4. a) fourth
    b) fourteenth

5. a) eighth
    b) eighteenth

6. a) seventh
    b) seventeenth

7. a) twenty-second
    b) second

8. a) sixteenth
    b) fourteenth

9. a) eleventh
    b) eighth

10. a) fifteenth
     b) twenty-fifth

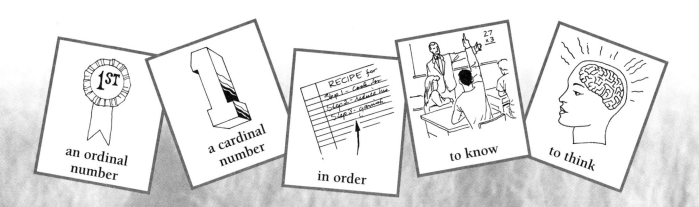

an ordinal number

a cardinal number

in order

to know

to think

C Listen to the teacher. Circle the numbers you hear. Use the worksheet.

1. a) 8th   6. a) 21st
    b) 18th   b) 1st

2. a) 9th   7. a) 11th
    b) 29th   b) 21st

3. a) 15th   8. a) 2nd
    b) 25th   b) 3rd

4. a) 16th   9. a) 4th
    b) 14th   b) 14th

5. a) 20th   10. a) 25th
    b) 10th   b) 5th

D Complete the sentences with ordinal numbers.

> March is the **third** month of the year.

1. July is the _____ month of the year.

2. September is the _____ month of the year.

3. The fourth month of the year is _____.

4. The twelfth month of the year is _____.

5. November is the _____ month of the year.

6. The second month of the year is _____.

7. May is the _____ month of the year.

8. The eighth month of the year is _____.

9. The _____ month of the year is February.

10. April is the _____ month of the year.

11. The ninth month of the year is _____.

12. October is the _____ month of the year.

to smile   to laugh   to cry   to need   to watch

BIRTHDAYS

A Look.

B Write the date (month and day) of your birthday.

My birthday is _____.

C Talk with five students. Make a chart and write the dates.

Ask: When is your birthday?

Answer: My birthday is _____.

Name	Birthday
1.	
2.	
3.	
4.	
5.	

a birthday party   a cake   candles   to blow   to sing

HOW OLD ARE YOU?

A   Practise with the teacher.

to cut

to serve

to eat

to give

presents

B   Copy the second chart. Complete the chart.

Name	Age	Birthday
Max Kuslov	31 years old	January 15th
Olga Kuslov	30 years old	July 14th
Michel Banon	25 years old	April 11th
Lili Han	28 years old	March 1st
Mona Aziz	22 years old	September 16th
Carlos Lopez	35 years old	February 20th
Ana Lopez	29 years old	September 16th
Kate Martin	28 years old	June 4th
Jun Kim	23 years old	August 20th

First name	Family name	Age	Birthday
Ana		29	September
	Kim		20th
	Banon	25	April 11th
Olga			July
Lili	Han		1st
	Martin	28	June 4th
Max		31	15th
Mona		22	September
	Lopez		February 20th

C   Answer "yes" or "no."

1. Lili is 21 years old.   Yes   No

2. Max's birthday is January 15th.   Yes   No

3. Mona is 22 years old.   Yes   No

4. Carlos is 36 years old.   Yes   No

5. Olga's birthday is July 14th.   Yes   No

6. Michel is 27 years old.   Yes   No

7. Jun is 26 years old.   Yes   No

8. Kate's birthday is July 4th.   Yes   No

to receive   to open   to thank   to kiss   to hug

GRAMMAR FOCUS   Asking Questions

To ask questions with **be**, put the verb before the subject. Put a question mark(?) at the end of the subject.

> They are English.
> Are they English?

Am I	
Are you	
Is he	
Is she	
Is it	from Poland?
Are we	
Are you	
Are they	

A   Write questions.

> Kate is a teacher.   **Is Kate a teacher?**

1. Jun is a young man.
2. They are friends.
3. She is a teacher.
4. They are immigrants.
5. Carlos and Ana are married.
6. Michel is a cook.
7. We are good students.
8. Ana is single.
9. Mona is from here.
10. Lili is divorced.

11. Olga is a housewife.
12. Jun is from Korea.
13. She is a tourist.
14. They are students.
15. He is a taxi driver.
16. You are a student.
17. I am right.
18. She is an old woman.
19. You are from Korea.
20. We are wrong.

to put

To Go

a verb

? a question mark

a taxi driver

a cook

B Read the story. Answer the questions. Write "yes" or "no."

My name is Lili Han. I am from Shanghai. Shanghai is a city in China. It is very big. I am a young woman and I am divorced.

Now I am an immigrant. I am a student in an English class. My teacher is Kate. She is from Canada. The classroom is small.

1. Is her first name Han?

2. Is she from a big city?

3. Is Shanghai in China?

4. Is Lili married?

5. Is Lili a student in China?

6. Is Lili an old woman?

7. Is Kate a teacher?

8. Is Kate an immigrant?

9. Is Lili English?

10. Is the classroom big?

SORRY, WRONG NUMBER

LISTENING ACTIVITY 3

A Practise with the teacher.

Conversation 1

Woman: Hello.

Man: Hello. May I speak to Olga please?

Woman: I'm sorry. This is the wrong number.

Man: Oh, excuse me.

Woman: No problem.

the beginning   the end   an immigrant   a tourist   a housewife

Conversation 2

Man: Hello.

Woman: Hello. May I speak to Michel please?

Man: I'm sorry. This is the wrong number.

Woman: Oh, excuse me.

Man: No problem.

Conversation 3

Woman: Hello.

Man: Hello. May I speak to Jun please?

Woman: I'm sorry. This is the wrong number.

Man: Oh, excuse me.

Woman: No problem.

  B   Listen and complete. Use the worksheet.

Conversation 1

Woman: Hello.

Man: Hello. May I _____ to Max please?

Woman: I'm sorry. This is the _____ number.

Man: Oh, excuse me.

Woman: No problem.

Conversation 2

Man: Hello.

Woman: Hello. _____ I speak to Kate please?

Man: I'm sorry. _____ is the wrong number.

Woman: Oh, excuse me.

Man: _____ problem.

to ring   to call   to dial   to wait   to hang up

Conversation 3

Woman:	Hello.
Man:	Hello. May _____ speak to Ana please?
Woman:	I'm sorry. This _____ the wrong number.
Man:	Oh, _____ me.
Woman:	No problem.

Conversation 4

Man:	Hello.
Woman:	Hello. May I speak _____ Mona please?
Man:	I'm _____. This is the wrong number.
Woman:	Oh, excuse _____.
Man:	No problem.

  C Practise the conversations with a partner.

to go   to run   to stop   to enter   to leave

WORD REVIEW

Write the words for the pictures.

a birthday party

a calendar

a cardinal number

a cook

a day

a housewife

a month

a question mark

a taxi driver

a week

a year

an abbreviation

an ordinal number

to call

to cry

to eat

to ring

to smile

to study

to watch

WHERE ARE YOU FROM?

SPELL THE COUNTRY

A   Listen to the teacher. Write the country. Use your notebook.

Canada   **C A N A D A**

B   Match the countries to the map.

Haiti
Greece
Egypt
Mexico
Japan
Russia
Brazil
Italy
China
Poland
Korea
Somalia
France
Malaysia
Peru

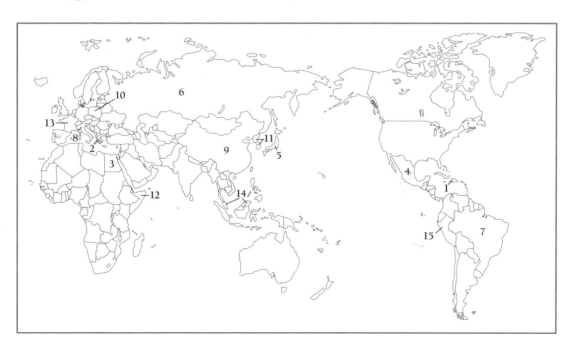

WHERE ARE THEY FROM?

A   Look at the pictures and practise with the teacher.

B   Listen to the teacher. Complete the sentences. Use the worksheet.

1.   Hi. My name is Mona. I _____ from Egypt.

2.   Hello. My name _____ Ana. I am from Mexico.

3.   Hi. I'm Max. I' _____ from Russia.

4.   Hello. My name is Jun. I am _____ Korea.

5.   Hello. My name is Lili. I' _____ from China.

6.   Hi. I' _____ Michel. I'm _____ Haiti.

7.   Hi. I'm Carlos. I _____ from Mexico.

8.   Hello. I' _____ Kate. I'm from here.

a country

a city

an address

a phone number

a postal code

WHERE ARE YOU FROM?

LISTENING ACTIVITY 4

A Practise with the teacher.

Conversation 1

Kate: Where are you from?

Jun: I am from Korea. And you?

Kate: I'm from here.

Conversation 2

Carlos: Where are you from?

Max: I am from Russia. And you?

Carlos: Ana and I are from Mexico.

Conversation 3

Lili: Where are you from?

Kate: I'm from here. And you?

Lili: I am from China.

Conversation 4

Michel: Where are you from?

Lili: I'm from Mexico. And you?

Michel: I am from Haiti.

Conversation 5

Olga: Where are you from?

Mona: I'm from Egypt. And you?

Olga: I'm from Russia.

an apartment number   a tree   flowers   grass   a fence

B Listen and write the words. Use the worksheet.

Conversation 1

Mona: Where are you _____from_____ ?

Lili: I _____from_____ from China. And you?

Mona: I _____from_____ from Egypt.

Conversation 2

Olga: Where _____are_____ you from, Carlos?

Carlos: I am from Mexico. And _____you_____ ?

Olga: Max and I are _____from_____ Russia.

Conversation 3

Ana: Where are you from, Kate?

Kate: I'm from Canada. Where are you _____from_____ ?

Ana: I _____from_____ from Mexico.

Conversation 4

Michel: Where _____are_____ you from, Kate?

Kate: I am _____ here. And you?

Michel: I _____am_____ from Haiti.

Conversation 5

Jun: Where _____are_____ you from, Ana?

Ana: I _____am_____ from Mexico. And _____you_____ ?

Jun: I am _____from_____ Korea.

C Practise the conversations with a partner.

a mailbox

a telephone booth

traffic lights

a stop sign

a crosswalk

D Copy the chart. Talk to five students. Ask and answer the questions. Complete the chart.

Where are you from?

I am from _____.

Name	Country
1.	
2.	
3.	
4.	
5.	

GRAMMAR FOCUS

Verb "Be" Negative

Use **not** after **be**.

We are tired

We are **not** tired.

a bus stop

a gas station

a parking meter

a restaurant

a bank

Full form	Contraction A	Contraction B
I am not	I'm not	
you are not	you're not	you aren't
he is not	he's not	he isn't
she is not	she's not	she isn't
it is not	it's not	it isn't
we are not	we're not	we aren't
you are not	you're not	you aren't
they are not	they're not	they aren't

 A   Make the sentences negative. Use Contraction A.

> I am a student.   **I'm not a student.**

1.   Kate is from China.

2.   China is a small country.

3.   Michel is from Korea.

4.   Olga is from Mexico.

5.   Jun is from a big country.

6.   Max and Olga are from China.

7.   Mexico is a cold country.

8.   Ana and Carlos are from Egypt.

9.   England is a big country.

10.   Michel is from a cold country.

11.   Egypt is a new country.

12.   Mona is from Canada.

13.   Jun is from Russia.

14.   Lili is from Haiti.

15.   Canada is an old country.

hot   warm   cool   cold   freezing

B Write the contractions.

they are not	**they're not**

1. he is not
2. we are not
3. it is not
4. I am not
5. Jun is not

6. they are not
7. Ana is not
8. she is not
9. you are not
10. Kate is not

JOBS

A Look and practise with the teacher.

a teacher a doctor a nurse an orderly a job

Michel
a cook

Kate
a teacher

Mona
a nurse

Max
a taxi driver

Lili
a bank teller

Jun
an orderly

a bank teller

a taxi driver

a cook

a sales clerk

a cashier

B Match.

1. He's a taxi driver.   Jun

2. She's a bank teller.   Max

3. He's an orderly.   Kate

4. He's a cook.   Michel

5. She's a nurse.   Lili

6. She's a teacher.   Mona

C Make these sentences negative. Use Contraction B.

> Felix is a dog.   **Felix isn't a dog.**

1. Kate is a student.   6. Mona is a cook.

2. Olga and Ana are taxi drivers.   7. Ana is a teacher.

3. Michel is an orderly.   8. Max is an orderly.

4. Ana is a bank teller.   9. The students are old.

5. Carlos is a young man.   10. Olga and Max are teachers.

CANADIAN CAPSULES You can become a Canadian citizen after three years in Canada.

a mechanic   an electrician   a plumber   a janitor   an engineer

WHAT DO YOU DO?

LISTENING ACTIVITY 5

A   Listen and write the words. Use the worksheet.

Conversation 1

Max: Michel, what do you _____?

Michel: I'm a cook. And you? What _____ your job?

Max: I'm a taxi driver.

Conversation 2

Mona: What do you _____, Lili?

Lili: I'm a bank teller. What do _____ do, Mona?

Mona: I'm a nurse.

Conversation 3

Jun: _____ do you do, Olga?

Olga: I'm a student. What is your _____, Jun?

Jun: I'm an orderly.

B   Practise the conversations with a partner.

CANADIAN CAPSULES   The Aboriginal Peoples of Canada are the Inuit of the Arctic and the First Nations of other parts of Canada.

a secretary

an accountant

a hockey player

a photographer

a pilot

THE PICTURE GAME

A Look at the pictures. Answer the questions on page 74.

a flight attendant

a letter carrier

a server

a dentist

a hairdresser

B   Choose the answers.

1.	Are they married?	Yes, they are.	No, they aren't.
2.	Is Lili a cook?	Yes, she is.	No, she isn't.
3.	Is Kate a teacher?	Yes, she is.	No, she isn't.
4.	Is Max a taxi driver?	Yes, he is.	No, he isn't.
5.	Is she 20 years old?	Yes, she is.	No, she isn't.
6.	Are they old?	Yes, they are.	No, they aren't.
7.	Are they happy?	Yes, they are.	No, they aren't.
8.	Are they cold?	Yes, they are.	No, they aren't.
9.	Is he a cook?	Yes, he is.	No, he isn't.
10.	Is she sad?	Yes, she is.	No, she isn't.
11.	Is it big?	Yes, it is.	No, it isn't.
12.	Are you tired?	Yes, I am.	No, I'm not.

JOURNAL

A   Read the story.

My name is Jun Kim. I am from Korea. I am a man. I am not married. I am an orderly. I am in an English class.

B   Write five or six sentences about you.

a pharmacist

a day-care worker

a bus driver

a secretary

a cashier

WORD REVIEW

Write the words for the pictures.

a bank	
a bank teller	
a bus driver	
a cashier	
a city	
a country	
a dentist	
a doctor	
a nurse	
a phone number	
a restaurant	
a sales clerk	
a stop sign	
a taxi driver	
a teacher	
a tree	
an address	
an apartment number	
a postal code	
an orderly	

UNIT 6

WHAT TIME IS IT?

WHAT TIME IS IT?

 A Practise with the teacher.

77

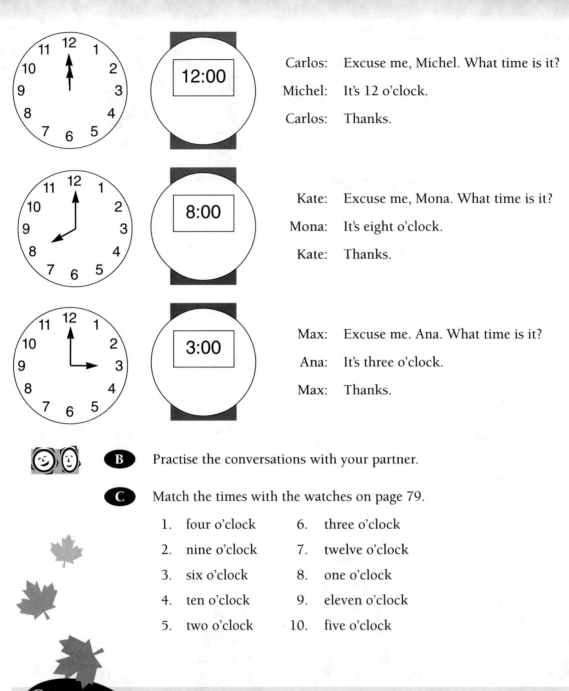

Carlos: Excuse me, Michel. What time is it?

Michel: It's 12 o'clock.

Carlos: Thanks.

Kate: Excuse me, Mona. What time is it?

Mona: It's eight o'clock.

Kate: Thanks.

Max: Excuse me. Ana. What time is it?

Ana: It's three o'clock.

Max: Thanks.

B   Practise the conversations with your partner.

C   Match the times with the watches on page 79.

1.   four o'clock   6.   three o'clock

2.   nine o'clock   7.   twelve o'clock

3.   six o'clock   8.   one o'clock

4.   ten o'clock   9.   eleven o'clock

5.   two o'clock   10.   five o'clock

CANADIAN CAPSULES   It is very important to be on time for business meetings in Canada.

a clock   a business meeting   ten o'clock   five past ten   ten past ten

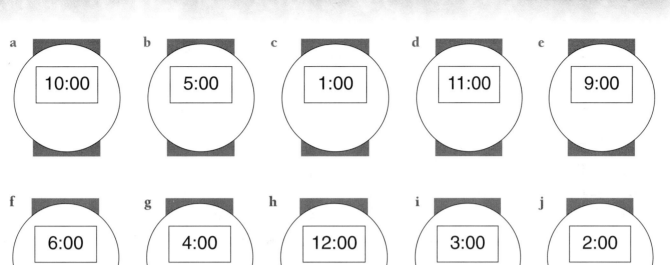

a 10:00

b 5:00

c 1:00

d 11:00

e 9:00

f 6:00

g 4:00

h 12:00

i 3:00

j 2:00

D Write the times. Use your notebook.

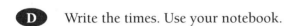

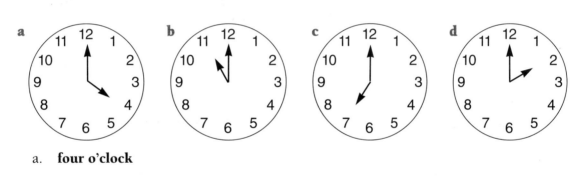

a b c d

a. **four o'clock**

e f g h

a quarter past ten

twenty past ten

twenty-five past ten

half past ten

twenty-five to eleven

TELLING TIME

A   Practise with the teacher.

| 9:00 | 9:15 | 9:30 | 9:45 |
| It's nine o'clock. | It's a quarter past nine. | It's half past nine. | It's a quarter to ten. |

| 9:05 | 9:10 | 9:20 | 9:25 |
| It's five past nine. | It's ten past nine. | It's twenty past nine. | It's twenty-five past nine. |

   B   Practise with a partner. Say the times.

6:05

It's five past six.

twenty to eleven   a quarter to eleven   ten to eleven   five to eleven   eleven o'clock

C   Practise with the teacher.

4:35
It's twenty-five to five.

4:40
It's twenty to five.

4:50
It's ten to five.

4:55
It's five to five.

to wake up   early   late   the sun   sunrise

D   Draw the times on the clocks. Use the worksheet.

1. twenty to seven   4. a quarter to eleven

2. five to eight   5. twenty-five to ten

3. ten to six   6. a quarter to two

It's noon   It's midnight.

CANADIAN CAPSULES   Most Canadians use an alarm clock to wake up every day.

morning   noon   afternoon   evening   night

TIME ZONES

A Look at the map of Canada.

B Answer the questions.

1. It's ten o'clock in Vancouver. What time is it in Toronto?

2. It's two o'clock in Halifax. What time is it in Montreal?

3. It's eight o'clock in Winnipeg. What time is it in St. John's?

4. It's noon in Montreal. What time is it in Vancouver?

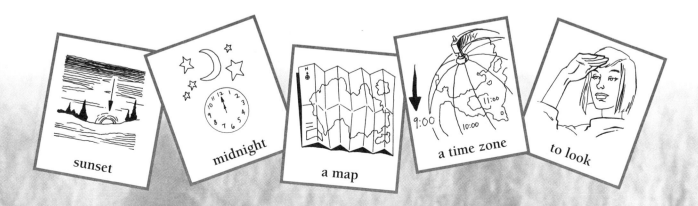

sunset   midnight   a map   a time zone   to look

5. It's six o'clock in Regina. What time is it in Halifax?

6. It's eleven o'clock in Toronto. What time is it in Edmonton?

7. It's midnight in Montreal. What time is it in Winnipeg?

8. It's one o'clock in Calgary. What time is it in Toronto?

9. It's three o'clock in Vancouver. What time is it in Calgary?

10. It's four o'clock in Montreal. What time is it in Halifax?

IS THAT A NEW WATCH?

LISTENING ACTIVITY 6

A   Practise with the teacher.

Conversation 1

Max:	Hi Mona. Is that a new watch?
Mona:	Yes, it is.
Max:	Is it a digital watch?
Mona:	Yes, it is.
Max:	What time is it?
Mona:	It's ten-forty-five.

10:45

Conversation 2

Ana:	Hi Jun. Is that a new watch?
Jun:	Yes, it is.
Ana:	Is it a digital watch?
Jun:	Yes, it is.
Ana:	What time is it?
Jun:	It's three-ten.

3:10

new   old   a watch   a digital watch   batteries

B Listen and write the words.

Conversation 1

Kate: Hi Carlos. Is that __a__ new watch?

Carlos: Yes, it is.

Kate: __Is__ it a digital watch?

Carlos: Yes, __it__ is.

Kate: What time is it?

Carlos: __It__'s eleven o five.

11:05

Conversation 2

Olga: Hi Michel. Is that a new watch?

Michel: Yes, it __is__.

Olga: Is it a digital watch?

Michel: Yes, __it__ is.

Olga: What time is it?

Michel: It's __three__ forty.

3:40

   C Practise the conversations with a partner.

D Write the times the teacher says. Use your notebook.

| It is three fifteen. | **3:15** |

CANADIAN CAPSULES Banks and stores open and close at different times in different cities in Canada.

a store   to open   to close   the same   different

WHERE ARE THEY?

A   Look at the pictures. Match the people to the places.

1. at the bank
2. at the grocery store
3. at the drug store
4. at the post office

5. at the dentist
6. at the gas station
7. at school

➡

Ana

Carlos

Michel

Jun

B Answer the questions.

| Where are you? | **I am in class.** |

1. Where is Kate?
2. Where are Max and Olga?
3. Where is Mona?
4. Where is Lili?

5. Where are Carlos and Ana?
6. Where is Michel?
7. Where is Jun?

a supermarket

a restaurant

a shopping centre

a movie theatre

a park

FOLLOW MICHEL

 A   Look at the pictures. Write the places.

a

b

c

d

a hospital

a police station

a fire station

a church

a factory

B   Look at Michel's schedule. Put the pictures in order.

8:15	at the gas station	3:20	at the post office
8:40	at the drugstore	3:30	at the bank
9:00	at English class	3:45	at the supermarket
12:10	at the dentist	4:25	at home

a hotel   a cafe   a market   a school   a university

C   Talk with you partner. Use the pictures. Tell the story.

D   Complete the story of Michel's day.

It is eight ___**fifteen**___. Michel is __**at the gas station**__. It is
_____ and he is at the drugstore. It is nine _____
and he is with Jun. They are at _____.

It is _____. Michel is _____ dentist. It is three _____
and Michel is at __**the post office**__. Now Michel is at the _____.
It is _____.

Michel is at the _____. It is three _____. Now it is four
_____ and he is at __**home**__.

WHAT ARE THE HOURS?

A   Look at the picture. Look at the signs on page 91.

an hour

a sign

open

closed

a light

Banking Hours

Mon.	10 – 3
Tues.	10 – 3
Wed.	10 – 3
Thur.	10 – 6
Fri.	10 – 6
Sat.	closed
Sun.	closed

Post Office Hours

Mon.	9 – 6
Tues.	9 – 6
Wed.	9 – 6
Thur.	9 – 9
Fri.	9 – 9
Sat.	9 – 1
Sun.	closed

Supermarket Hours

Mon.	9 – 7
Tues.	9 – 7
Wed.	9 – 7
Thur.	9 – 9
Fri.	9 – 9
Sat.	9 – 5
Sun.	11 - 5

B Answer "Yes, it is" or "No, it isn't."

1. The bank is open at a quarter to nine on Monday.

2. The supermarket is closed at a quarter past eight on Tuesday.

3. The supermarket is open at six o'clock on Saturday.

4. The post office is closed at 10 o'clock on Sunday.

5. The bank is closed at 11 o'clock on Wednesday.

6. The post office is open at half past two on Saturday.

7. The supermarket is open at eight o'clock on Friday.

8. The post office is closed at a quarter to ten on Thursday.

9. The bank is open at half past five on Tuesday.

10. The supermarket is open at nine o'clock on Sunday.

a bank teller   a banking machine   a bank card   cash   to line up

I'M LATE

LISTENING ACTIVITY 7

A   Practise with the teacher.

Conversation 1

Olga: Hello, Max.

Max: Hi, Olga. Where are you?

Olga: I'm at the supermarket. What time is it?

Max: It's half past five.

Olga: Oh, I'm late. See you soon.

Conversation 2

Carlos: Hello, Ana.

Ana: Hi, Carlos. Where are you?

Carlos: I'm at the post office. What time is it?

Ana: It's a quarter past one.

Carlos: Oh, I'm late. See you soon.

Conversation 3

Lili: Hello, Mona.

Mona: Hi Lili. Where are you?

Lili: I'm at the bank. What time is it?

Mona: It's ten to two.

Lili: Oh, I'm late. See you soon.

 B   Practise the conversations with a partner.

a receipt   a personal identification number (P.I.N.)   to deposit   to withdraw   a cheque

C   Listen and choose the answer.

Conversation 1

1. Jun is at the
    a) gas station
    b) supermarket

2. It is
    a) ten to three
    b) ten past three

Conversation 2

1. Kate is at the
    a) post office
    b) drug store

2. It is
    a) a quarter to four
    b) a quarter past four

Conversation 3

1. Michel is at the
    a) supermarket
    b) post office

2. It is
    a) twenty-five to two
    b) five past two

a bill

to insert

to remove

an account

the balance

GRAMMAR
FOCUS

Possessive Nouns

To show possession, add apostrophe **s** ('s) after the noun.

> It is the teacher's pen.
>
> It is Kate's pen.

A   Match the pictures to the sentences.

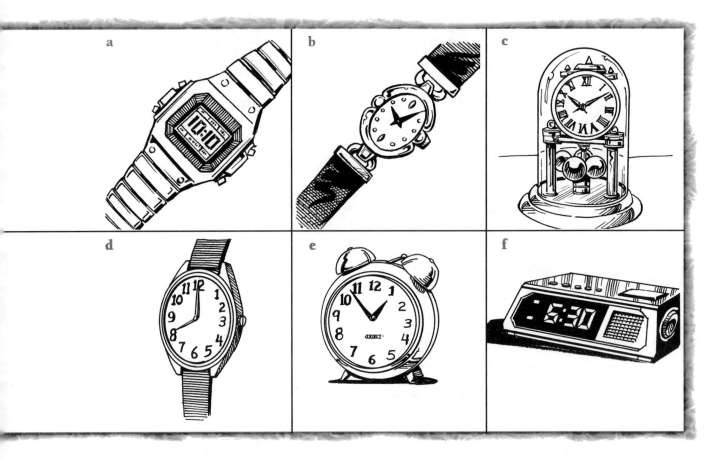

1. It's a man's watch.
2. It's an alarm clock.
3. It's a clock.

4. It's a woman's watch.
5. It's a clock-radio.
6. It's a digital watch.

a clock

an alarm clock

a watch

a digital watch

a clock radio

B Look around your classroom. Find these things. Write phrases.

> **the teacher's desk.**

1. pencils
2. books
3. desks

4. chairs
5. pens
6. paper

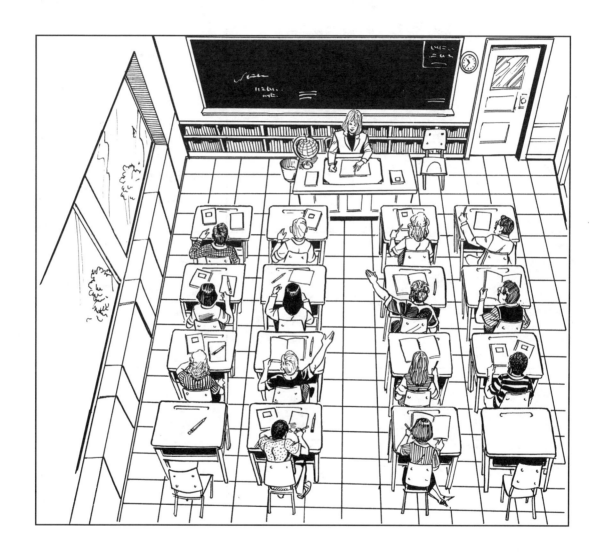

a classroom   a pen   a pencil   a desk   paper

WORD REVIEW

Write the words for the pictures.

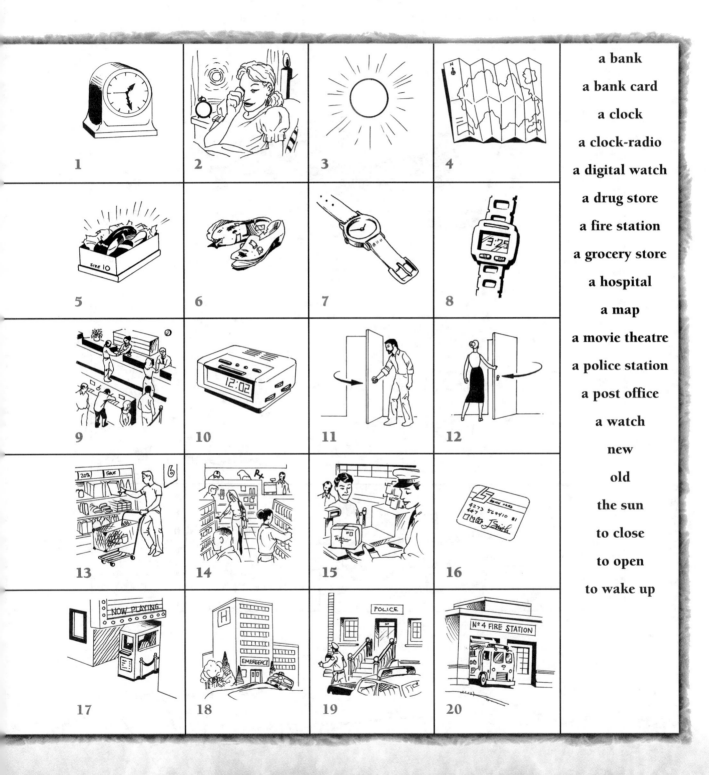

a bank

a bank card

a clock

a clock-radio

a digital watch

a drug store

a fire station

a grocery store

a hospital

a map

a movie theatre

a police station

a post office

a watch

new

old

the sun

to close

to open

to wake up

UNIT 7

WHERE DO YOU LIVE?

Mr. and Mrs. Max Kuslov
3684 Pine Avenue, Apt. 204
Vancouver, BC
Canada V8C 3E8

A   Practise with the teacher.

> 2435 Pine Avenue   Say: 24 35 Pine Avenue

1.   4025 Wilson Street
2.   7246 Peach Street
3.   1953 Maple Avenue
4.   3528 Milton Street
5.   4886 Fort Street
6.   615 Georgia Avenue
7.   8021 Beech Avenue
8.   919 Fraser Street
9.   2774 Tudor Road
10. 2859 Main Street
11. 627 River Road
12. 5647 Granville Street
13. 8978 Young Street
14. 2234 Portage Street
15. 928 Willow Street
16. 1655 Greene Avenue

B   Write the words for the numbers.

7468	**seventy four sixty eight**
614	**six fourteen**

1.   921
2.   1663
3.   4256
4.   6641
5.   4769
6.   2727
7.   3456
8.   802
9.   4653
10. 5756
11. 426
12. 8866
13. 2774
14. 605
15. 4025

CANADIAN CAPSULES   Canada has ten provinces and two territories. After 1999, there will be three territories.

a house   an apartment building   an address   an apartment number   a province

SAYING APARTMENT NUMBERS

A   Practise with the teacher.

> Apartment 604   Say: Apartment six o four

1. Apartment 1214
2. Apartment 308
3. Apartment 10
4. Apartment 906
5. Apartment 1104

6. Apartment 15
7. Apartment 101
8. Apartment 1002
9. Apartment 720
10. Apartment 12

B   Write the words for the apartment numbers.

> Apt. 602   **six o two**

1. Apt. 18
2. Apt. 906
3. Apt. 304
4. Apt. 8
5. Apt. 16

6. Apt. 201
7. Apt. 10
8. Apt. 520
9. Apt. 1813
10. Apt. 408

WHAT'S YOUR ADDRESS?

A   Practise with the teacher.

Conversation 1

Carlos: Hi Lili. What's your address?

Lili: My address is 2634 Milton Street.

Carlos: What's your apartment number?

Lili: It's apartment 504.

a territory   a mailbox   an elevator   stairs   a railing

Conversation 2

Olga: Hi Mona. What's your address?

Mona: My address is 308 Maple Street.

Olga: What is your apartment number?

Mona: It's number 1806.

Conversation 3

Jun: Hi Max. What's your address?

Max: My address is 3684 Pine Avenue.

Jun: What is your apartment number?

Max: It's apartment 204.

Conversation 4

Michel: Hi Carlos. What's your address?

Carlos: My address is 1953 Beech Street.

Michel: What is your apartment number?

Carlos: It's number 22.

 B   Practise with a partner.

C   Write your address. Use your notebook.

My address is _____ .

My apartment number is _____ .

 D   Write the address of three students in your class. Use your notebook.

Name:

Mr. / Ms. _____   _____
              Family name   First name

Address: _____

a door   a doorstep   a doorbell   to ring   a mat

PROVINCES

A Look at the map. Practise with the teacher.

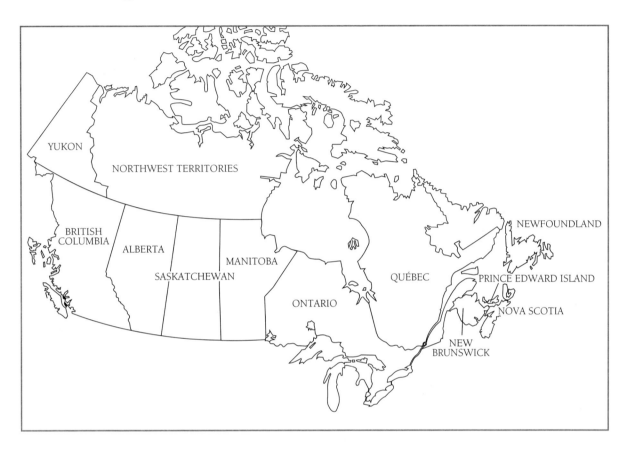

B Write the province or territory codes on the map. Use the worksheet.

| Ontario **ON** |

AB   NT

BC   PE

MA   QC

NB   SN

NS   YN

NF

a province code

a train

an airplane

a bus

a road

C   Copy the names and addresses. Add the province code for each address.

Mr. J. Black
6387 College Ave.
Calgary

Ms. Julie Braun
212 Wolfe St.
Vancouver

Mr. and Mrs. R. Silver
879 Peel St.
Montreal

Mr. Arthur Jones
7801 Pierce St.
Halifax

Ms. P. Salvi
5490 Regent St.
Toronto

CANADIAN CAPSULES   Street addresses in Canada use "Road," "Street," "Avenue," or "Drive."

a highway   a street sign   an envelope   a stamp   a mailbox

D   Write the names of the provinces and territories.

AB	**Alberta**

1. BC
2. QC
3. ON
4. SN
5. MA
6. NS

7. PE
8. YN
9. NW
10. NB
11. ND

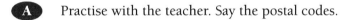

POSTAL CODES

A   Practise with the teacher. Say the postal codes.

1. H3T 1J6
2. V0R 2H0
3. K2C 3M6
4. J8X 3G1
5. A1E 2Y2

6. V5L 3B4
7. M1P 2P5
8. H4R 1T9
9. R3B 1NB
10. S7N 0W0

B   Practise with a partner. Say the postal codes.

1. J8X 3G1
2. V5L 3B4
3. M1P 2P5
4. S7N 0W0
5. K2C 3M6

6. H3T 1J6
7. A1E 2Y2
8. R3B 1NB
9. J8X 3G1
10. H3B 1C6

a return address   a package   string   tape   postcards

WHAT'S YOUR POSTAL CODE?

 Practise with the teacher.

Conversation 1

Ana: Oh Lili. What's your postal code?

Lili: It's H3T IJ6.

Ana: Is that H3T 1T6?

Lili: No. It's H3T 1J6.

Ana: OK. Thanks.

Conversation 2

Kate: Oh Jun. What's your postal code?

Jun: It's S3N 1T9

Kate: Is that STN 1T9?

Jun: No. It's S3N 1T9.

Kate: OK. Thanks.

Conversation 3

Carlos: Oh Kate. What's your postal code?

Kate: It's V5T 4N3.

Carlos: Is that V5G 4N3?

Kate: No. It's V5T 4N3.

Carlos: OK. Thanks.

Conversation 4

Jun: Oh Michel. What's your postal code?

Michel: It's M3P 5Y4

Jun: Is that M3T 5I4?

Michel: No. It's M3P 5Y4.

Jun: OK. Thanks.

to mail/to send   to receive   to sign   to pay   to open

D Practise the conversations with your partner.

E Ask your partner's postal code.

Partner A: Oh _____. What's your postal code?

Partner B: It's _____.

Partner A: It that _____?

Partner B: Yes/no. It's _____.

NAME AND ADDRESS

LISTENING ACTIVITY 8

A Read the conversation and complete the envelope. Use the worksheet.

```
                                    ┌──────┐
                                    │      │
                                    │      │
                                    └──────┘

Mr. Max K__slov
_____ Pine Avenue, Apt. 204
Vancouver, BC
Canada V8C _____
```

Clerk: Good morning sir. What's your name?

Max: Max Kuslov.

Clerk: Please spell your last name.

Max: K U S L O V

Clerk: And your address?

Max: 3684 Pine Avenue, Apt. 204
Vancouver, BC
Canada V8C 3E8

Clerk: Thanks.

 **CANADIAN CAPSULES** Postal codes in Canada use letter, number, letter; number, letter, number.

a letter   to write   to lick   a box   to carry

B   Listen and complete the envelopes. Use the worksheets.

1

Ms. Lili __an
49 _____ Fort Street, Apt. __
Winnipeg, Ma
Canada R3 __ 1N __

2

Mr. Carlos Lop____
____28 Maple Avenue, Apt.___
Toronto, ON
Canada __5P 4W2

3

Mr. Michel ____non
_____ Milton Avenue, Apt. __
Halifax, NS
Canada __4__ 3N5

4

Ms. Mona Az____
9_____ Willow Street, Apt. 4
Regina, SN
Canada S7N 4____

 C   Complete envelopes for you and your partner. Use the worksheet.

GIVING INFORMATION

A   Read the questions with the teacher.

1.   What is your last name?

2.   What is your telephone number?

3.   What is your postal code?

4.   Spell your family name, please.

5.   What is your apartment number?

6.   What is your first name?

7.   What is your address?

a family/last name

a first name

a telephone number

a postal code

an apartment number

B   Match the questions and answers.

1. What is your last name?   a) Kate
2. What is your telephone number?   b) H3T 1J6
3. What is your postal code?   c) Martin
4. Spell your family name, please.   d) It's number 406.
5. What is your apartment number?   e) 1624 Wilson Avenue
6. What is your first name?   f) 525-8610
7. What is your address?   g) M A R T I N

C   Write questions.

> **What's your address?**

1. 4286 Pine Street   3. Lopez   5. 736-2015
2. Apt. 27   4. Ana   6. M2P 1K5

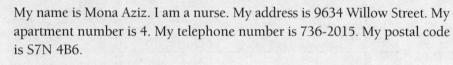

JOURNAL

A   Read the journal.

My name is Mona Aziz. I am a nurse. My address is 9634 Willow Street. My apartment number is 4. My telephone number is 736-2015. My postal code is S7N 4B6.

B   Write about you.

CANADIAN CAPSULES

The prime minister's residence is at 24 Sussex Drive, Ottawa.

an address

to spell

a prime minister

a residence

Ottawa

WORD REVIEW

Write the words for the pictures.

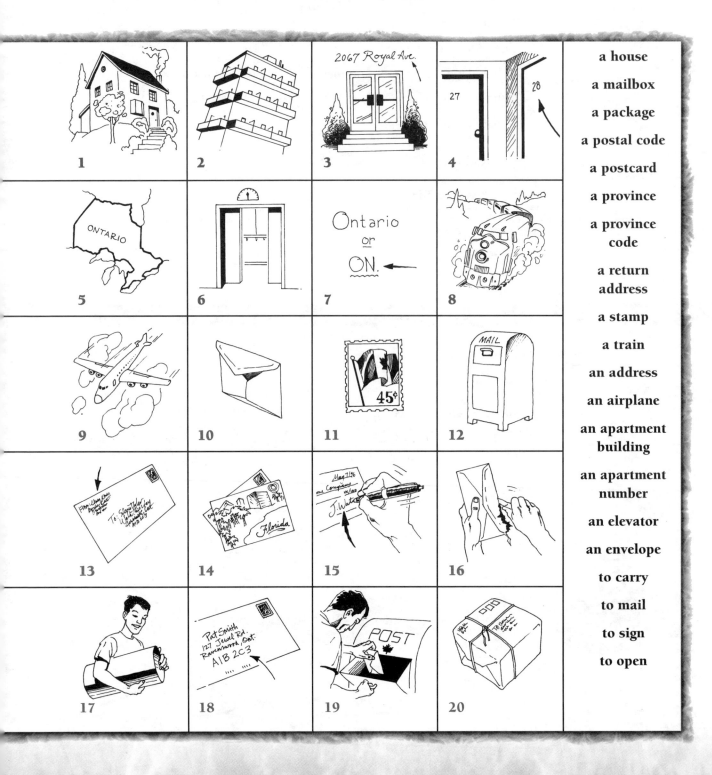

a house

a mailbox

a package

a postal code

a postcard

a province

a province code

a return address

a stamp

a train

an address

an airplane

an apartment building

an apartment number

an elevator

an envelope

to carry

to mail

to sign

to open

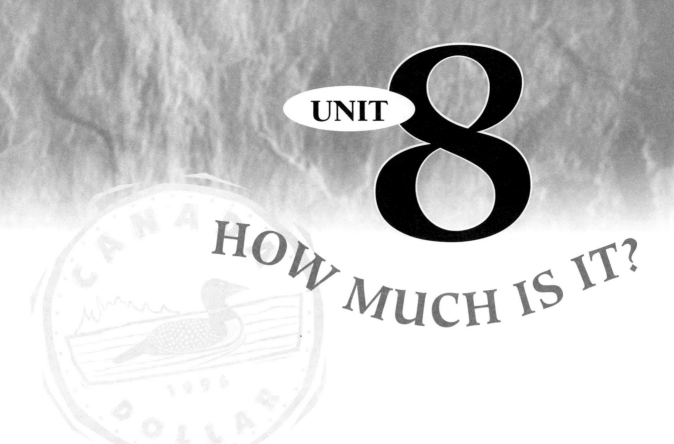

UNIT 8

HOW MUCH IS IT?

DOLLARS AND CENTS

A Look and practise with the teacher.

1 cent
OR a penny

5 cents
OR a nickel

10 cents
OR a dime

25 cents
OR a quarter

1 dollar
OR a loonie

a five-dollar bill

a twenty-dollar bill

2 dollars

a ten-dollar bill

a fifty-dollar bill

109

B   Practise with the teacher.

1¢ or $.01   5¢ or $.05   10¢ or $.10

25¢ or $.25 $1 or $1.00 $2 or $2.00

$5.00 $10.00

$20.00 $50.00

CANADIAN CAPSULES   The Canadian one-dollar coin is called a "loonie" because it has a picture of a loon on it. A loon is a bird.

a cent   five cents   ten cents   twenty-five cents   a dollar

C   Match the amounts to the coins.

a) 35¢

b) $2.02

c) 3¢

d) $2

e) 25¢

f) 20¢

g) 15¢

h) 75¢

i) 30¢

j) 14¢

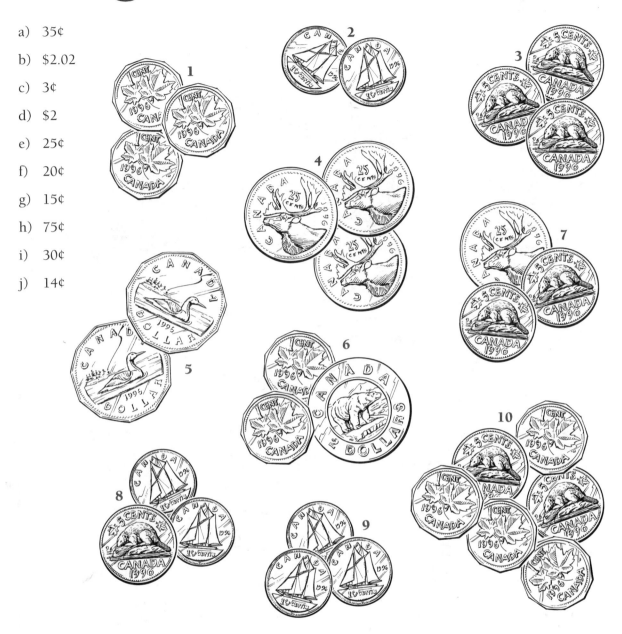

D   Listen and write the amounts you hear. Use your notebook.

$3.25

a maple leaf   a beaver   a sailboat/schooner   a caribou   a loon

WHERE IS MY MONEY?

A   Practise with the teacher.

in the bank

in my wallet

in my change purse

in my piggy bank

a polar bear

a bank

a wallet

a change purse

a piggy bank

B   Read and answer "yes" or "no."

Max has $300. It is in the bank. He has $15 in his wallet. He has a ten-dollar bill and a five-dollar bill.

Max has $1.87 in his change purse. He has a loonie, three quarters, a dime, and two pennies. He has money in his piggy bank. It is pennies, nickels, and dimes.

1. Max has $15 in his change purse.

2. Max has quarters in his piggy bank.

3. Max has $1.87 in his change purse.

4. Max has $300 in his wallet.

5. Max has bills in his piggy bank.

6. Max has nickels and dimes in the bank.

7. Max has a change purse and wallet.

8. Max has $400 in the bank.

9. Max has coins in his wallet.

10. Max has pennies in his change purse.

CANADIAN CAPSULES   People sometimes call dollars "bucks."

a purse   a pocket   to count   to buy   to save

COUNTING MONEY

A   Write the amounts.

$1.50

a cent

five cents

ten cents

twenty-five cents

a dollar

B Listen to the teacher. Circle the amount you hear. Use the worksheet.

1. a) $3.60
    b) $3.16

2. a) $.25
    b) $25

3. a) $1.57
    b) $1.07

4. a) $70
    b) $17

5. a) $1.61
    b) 61¢

6. a) $2.99
    b) $29.99

7. a) $5.35
    b) $5.55

8. a) $21.98
    b) $20.18

a two-dollar coin

a five-dollar bill

a ten-dollar bill

a twenty-dollar bill

a fifty-dollar bill

C   Listen to the teacher. Circle the amount you hear. Use the worksheet.

1. a)   b)

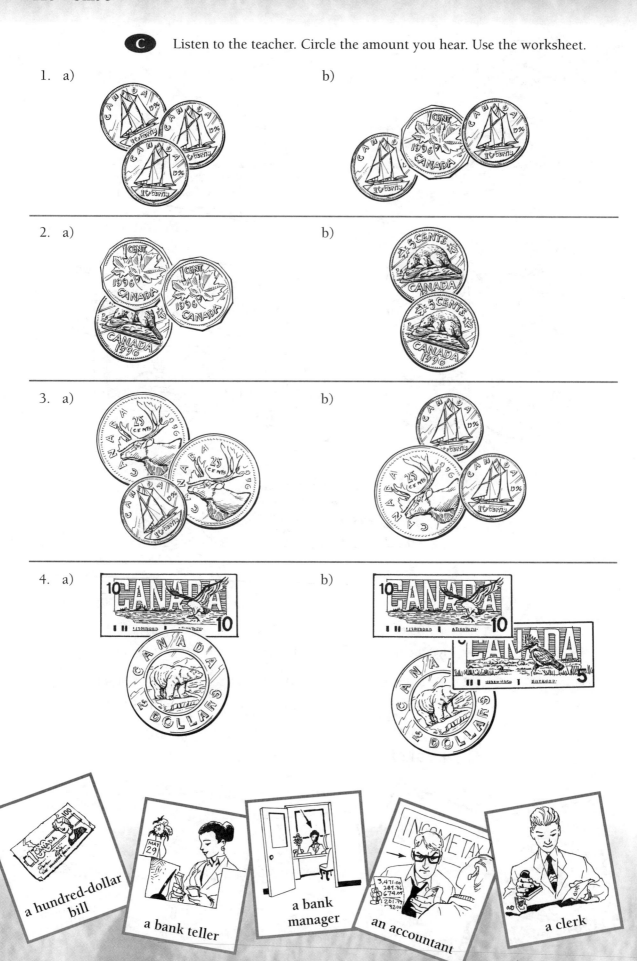

2. a)   b)

3. a)   b)

4. a)   b)

a hundred-dollar
bill

a bank teller

a bank
manager

an accountant

a clerk

5. a)

    b)

6. a)

    b)

7. a)

    b)

8. a)

    b)

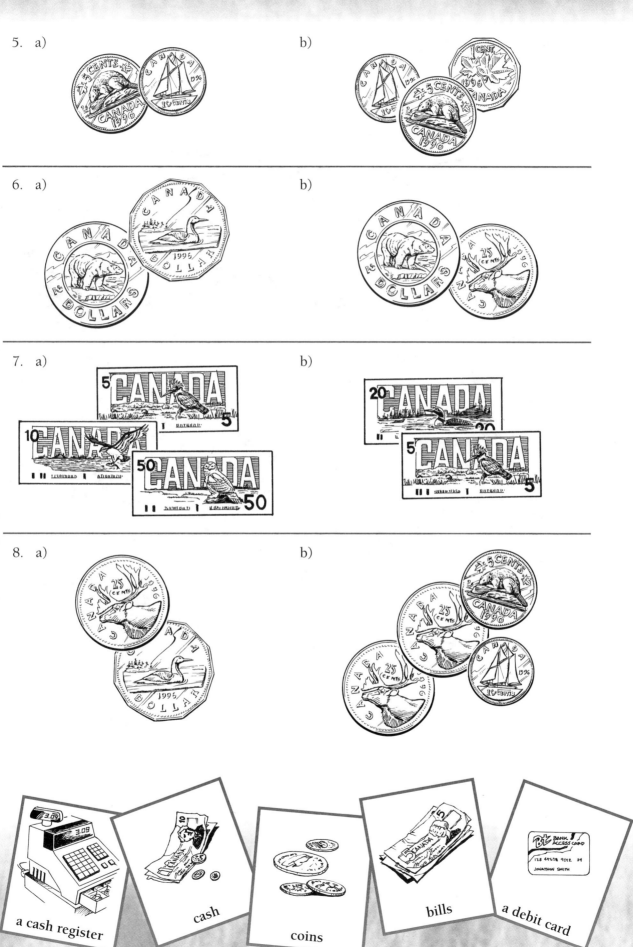

a cash register

cash

coins

bills

a debit card

AT THE SUPERMARKET

A   Practise with the teacher.

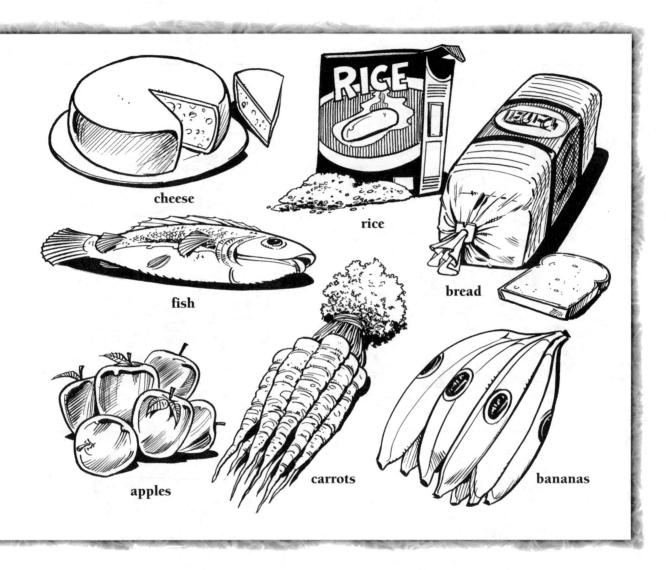

cheese

rice

bread

fish

apples

carrots

bananas

cheese

rice

bread

fish

an apple

B   Practise with a partner. Say the amounts.

C   Read the questions. Write the amounts in your notebook.

1. How much is the cheese?
2. How much is the fish?
3. How much are the apples?
4. How much are the carrots?

5. How much is the rice?
6. How much is the bread?
7. How much are the bananas?

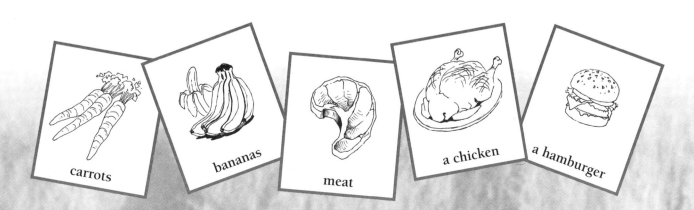

carrots   bananas   meat   a chicken   a hamburger

D   Copy the chart on page 121. Write the prices of the foods.

oranges

pears

peaches

strawberries

grapes

Bay Supermarket		Mario's Market
bananas	$1.39	$1.36
cheese		
apples		
bread		
rice		
fish		

HOW MUCH IS IT?

LISTENING ACTIVITY 9

A Practise with the teacher.

Conversation 1

Jun: Excuse me. How much are these bananas?

Clerk: They are $1.57.

Jun: And how much are the apples?

Clerk: They are $2.50

Jun: Thank you.

Clerk: You're welcome.

Conversation 2

Ana: Excuse me. How much is this bread?

Clerk: It's $1.65.

Ana: And how much is the rice?

Clerk: It's $1.19

Ana: Thank you.

Clerk: You're welcome.

lettuce   a pepper   celery   a cucumber   tomatoes

Conversation 3

Carlos: Excuse me. How much are these carrots?

Clerk: They are $1.29.

Carlos: And how much are the apples?

Clerk: They are $2.56

Carlos: Thank you.

Clerk: You're welcome.

Conversation 4

Mona: Excuse me. How much is this cheese?

Clerk: It's $4.65.

Mona: And how much is the fish?

Clerk: It's $3.89

Mona: Thank you.

Clerk: You're welcome.

 B Practise the conversations with a partner.

 C Listen and write the words. Use the worksheet.

Conversation 1

Olga: Excuse me. How much is the fish?

Clerk: It's _____.

Olga: And how much are the carrots?

Clerk: They are _____.

Olga: Thank you.

Clerk: You're welcome.

potatoes

broccoli

cauliflower

cereal

milk

Conversation 2

Michel: Excuse me. How much is this cheese?

Clerk: It's _____.

Michel: And how much _____ the apples?

Clerk: They are _____.

Michel: Thank you.

Clerk: You're welcome.

Conversation 3

Kate: Excuse me. How much is this rice?

Clerk: It's _____.

Kate: And how much _____ the bananas?

Clerk: They are _____.

Kate: Thank you.

Clerk: You're welcome.

  D   Practise the conversations with a partner.

potato chips   ice cream   cookies   cake   pie

WORD REVIEW

Write the words for the pictures.

1	2	3	4	a bank
5	6	7	8	a cent
9	10	11	12	a change purse
13	14	15	16	a dollar
17	18	19	20	a piggy bank

a bank

a cent

a change purse

a dollar

a piggy bank

a pocket

a purse

a wallet

an apple

bananas

bread

carrots

cheese

fish

five cents

rice

ten cents

to buy

to count

twenty-five cents

UNIT 9

MY FAMILY

KATE'S FAMILY

A   Look at Kate's family.

Anne
mother

John
father

Maria
sister

Kate

Joseph
brother

125

B   Read about Kate's family.

I'm Kate. This is my family. My mother is Anne. My father is John. My brother is Joseph. My sister is Maria.

C   Match the people.

1. mother   a) Kate
2. father   b) Maria
3. me   c) John
4. sister   d) Joseph
5. brother   e) Anne

THE AZIZ FAMILY

A   Look at the Aziz family.

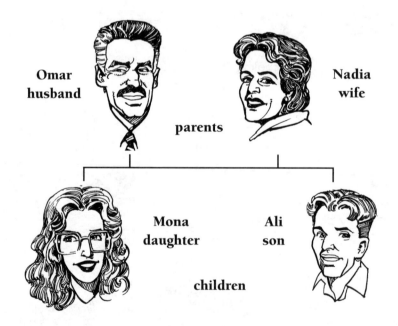

Omar
husband

Nadia
wife

parents

Mona
daughter

Ali
son

children

a family

a mother

a father

a brother

a sister

B   Read the story. Complete the sentences.

Omar and Nadia are married. Omar's wife is Nadia. Nadia's husband is Omar. They are Mona's parents. They have two children. Mona is their daughter. Ali is their son.

1. Nadia is Omar's _____.
2. Nadia's son is _____.
3. Omar's daughter is _____.
4. Ali is Omar's _____.
5. Nadia is Ali's _____.
6. Mona and Ali are Omar's _____.
7. Omar is Nadia's _____.
8. Omar and Nadia are Ali's _____.

OLGA AND MAX

A   Read about Olga and Max. Use the words to complete the story.

Olga

Max

Masha

married
daughter
wife
parents
husband

Olga: I'm Olga. This is my _____ Max. We are _____.
        Masha is our _____.

Max: I'm Max. Olga is my _____. Our daughter is Masha. We are
        Masha's _____.

a husband   a wife   a son   a daughter   a child

B　Match the opposites.

1.	husband	a)	male
2.	mother	b)	parents
3.	son	c)	wife
4.	girl	d)	sister
5.	man	e)	boy
6.	female	f)	woman
7.	children	g)	daughter
8.	brother	h)	father

JOURNAL

A　Read the story.

I'm Ana Lopez. This is my family. My husband is Carlos. My mother is Susana. My father is Alvaro.

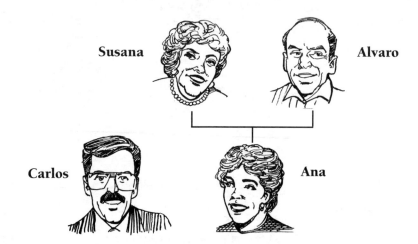

Susana　　**Alvaro**

Carlos　　**Ana**

B　Write about your family.

children　　male　　female　　parents　　grandparents

WHO'S IN THE FAMILY?

LISTENING ACTIVITY 10

A   Practise with the teacher. Then practise with a partner.

Conversation 1

Michel: Is this your family, Carlos?

Carlos: Yes, it is.

Michel: Who's that?

Carlos: That's my wife Ana.

a grandmother   a grandfather   a grandson   a grand-daughter   grandchildren

Conversation 2

Lili: Is this your family, Olga?

Olga: Yes it is.

Lili: Who's this?

Olga: It's my husband Max.

Lili: And who's this?

Olga: That's my daughter Masha.

Conversation 3

Ana: Is this your family, Kate?

Kate: Yes, it is.

Ana: Who's that?

Kate: That's my mother and my father.

Ana: And who's this?

Kate: This is my brother, and this is my sister.

 B   Listen and write the words. Use the worksheet.

Conversation 1

Mona: Is this your family, Lili?

Lili: Yes, it _____ , Mona.

Mona: Who's this?

Lili: That's my mother, and that's my _____ .

Mona: And who's this?

Lili: That's my _____ Amy.

a picture   to like   to love   to kiss   to hug

Conversation 2

Kate: Is this your family, Michel?

Michel: _____, it is, Kate.

Kate: Who are these people?

Michel: These are my _____.

Kate: And who are those people?

Michel: Those are my _____.

Conversation 3

Jun: Is this your _____, Mona?

Mona: Yes, it is, Jun.

Jun: Who's this?

Mona: This is my _____ Ali.

Jun: And who's this?

Mona: This is my _____, and this is my father.

 C Read the conversations with a partner.

 D Draw your family tree. Talk about your family.

young   old   to help   a tree   a family tree

Bob + Nancy
|
Maria + Warren
Jean   Sam

GRAMMAR FOCUS   Verb "Have"

A Write **have** or **has**.

I have
you have
he has
she has
it has
we have
you have
they have

1. Olga _____ a husband.

2. Olga and Max _____ a daughter.

3. Mona _____ a brother.

4. Kate _____ a sister.

5. Anne and John _____ three children.

6. Vancouver _____ rainy weather.

7. Toronto _____ hot summers.

8. Mona _____ a cat.

9. Kate and Maria _____ a brother.

10. Masha _____ two parents.

B Read the sentences. If the verb is wrong, correct it.

They has a dog.   **They have a dog.**

1. They have two children. ✓

2. Kate have a sister. ✗

3. Mexico has hot weather. ✓

4. I have a daughter. ✓

5. The classroom has two doors. ✗

6. We have new books. ✓

7. Mona have a brother. ✗

8. He has a son. ✓

9. Max has a wife. ✓

10. The class have fifteen students. ✓

spring   summer   fall/autumn   winter   hot

PEOPLE AROUND US

 Look at the picture. Practise the words with the teacher.

long hair

short hair

brown hair

black hair

a moustache

a beard

blond hair

blue eyes

brown eyes

glasses

tall   medium height   short   heavy   average   thin

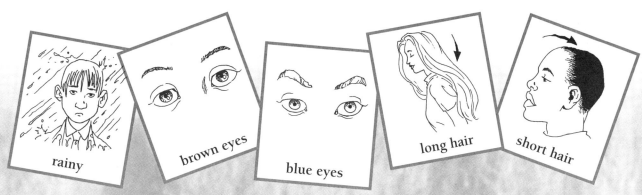

rainy   brown eyes   blue eyes   long hair   short hair

B Look at the pictures. Read the sentences on page 135. Write the names of the people.

Karen

Jim

Mike

Jeff

Peter

Nina

Steve

Lea

Kevin

Dina

black hair

brown hair

blond hair

tall

medium height

Marta   Victor   Marc   Jill   Henry

1. A husband and wife have a baby.

2. A girl has long brown hair.

3. A man has a beard and a moustache.

4. Lea has a husband.

5. A tall girl has two young brothers.

6. A young boy has glasses.

7. A young man has a moustache.

8. A man has a daughter.

9. Two children have blond hair.

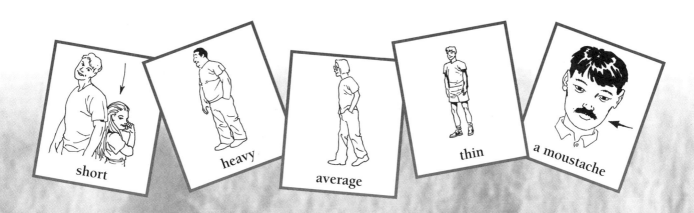

short   heavy   average   thin   a moustache

STUDENTS IN THE CLASS

A   Look at the people. Make a chart and put a check (✔) for each person.

	Kate	Mona	Michel	Jun
brown eyes		✔	✔	✔
blue eyes				
black hair				
brown hair				
blond hair				
glasses				
a beard				
a moustache				

a beard   glasses   curly hair   wavy hair   straight hair

B   Read about the people. Answer "yes" or "no."

1.   I'm Kate Martin. I'm a teacher. I have short blond hair and blue eyes. I'm medium height. I have a sister and a brother. My sister is medium height too. My brother is tall and thin.

1.	Kate is a teacher.	Yes	No
2.	Kate is tall.	Yes	No
3.	Kate has two brothers.	Yes	No
4.	Kate's sister is short.	Yes	No
5.	Kate's brother is tall and thin.	Yes	No

2.   Lili Han has long black hair. She is not tall. She is short. Her mother and father are also short. Lili has a sister. Her sister has glasses. Her father has glasses too.

1.	Lili has black hair.	Yes	No
2.	Lili is medium height.	Yes	No
3.	Lili's mother and father are short.	Yes	No
4.	Lili has glasses.	Yes	No
5.	Her father has glasses.	Yes	No

3.   Michel Banon is tall and thin. His father is tall and heavy. His mother is not heavy. Her weight is average. Michel has black hair and brown eyes. He has a beard and a moustache. His father has a beard and a moustache too.

1.	Michel Banon is heavy.	Yes	No
2.	Michel's father is heavy.	Yes	No
3.	His mother's weight is average.	Yes	No
4.	Michel has blue eyes.	Yes	No
5.	Michel's father has a beard.	Yes	No

bald   a face   a head   a mouth   a nose

4.   I'm Olga. I'm medium height, and I have brown hair and brown eyes. My husband is Max. He's tall and he has a moustache. Our daughter Masha has blond hair. Her hair is long.

1.	Olga is tall.	Yes	No
2.	Olga has brown hair.	Yes	No
3.	Olga has a moustache.	Yes	No
4.	Masha has brown hair.	Yes	No
5.	Masha has long hair.	Yes	No

C   Write a story about you and your family.

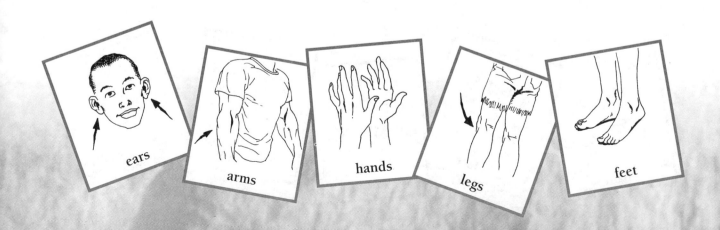

ears   arms   hands   legs   feet

WORD REVIEW

Write the words for the pictures.

a beard
a brother
a daughter
a family
a father
a husband
a mother
a moustache
a picture
a sister
a son
a tree
a wife
glasses
grandparents
long hair
parents
short
short hair
tall

10

HOW'S THE WEATHER?

THE WEATHER

A Look at the pictures. Practise the expressions on page 142 with the teacher.

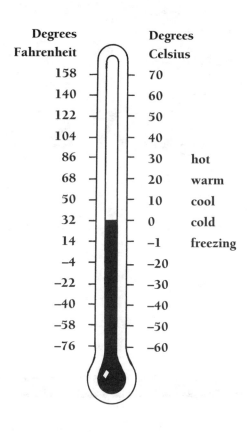

Degrees Fahrenheit	Degrees Celsius	
158	70	
140	60	
122	50	
104	40	
86	30	hot
68	20	warm
50	10	cool
32	0	cold
14	−1	freezing
−4	−20	
−22	−30	
−40	−40	
−58	−50	
−76	−60	

1. It's warm.
2. It's hot.
3. It's sunny.
4. It's cool.
5. It's cold.

6. It's windy.
7. It's rainy.
8. It's snowy.
9. It's freezing.

hot   warm   cool   cold   sunny

B   Look at the map. Answer the questions. Write "Yes it is" or "No it isn't."

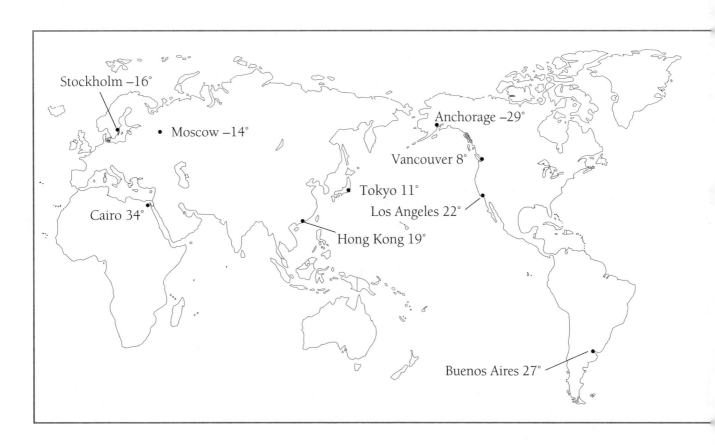

Stockholm –16°
Moscow –14°
Anchorage –29°
Vancouver 8°
Tokyo 11°
Los Angeles 22°
Cairo 34°
Hong Kong 19°
Buenos Aires 27°

1. Is it hot in Cairo?

2. Is it warm in Anchorage?

3. Is it cool in Stockholm?

4. Is it freezing in Moscow?

5. Is it hot in Tokyo?

6. Is it warm in Buenos Aires?

7. Is it cold in Los Angeles?

8. Is it freezing in Anchorage?

9. Is it cool in Vancouver?

10. Is it warm in Hong Kong?

windy

rainy

snowy

freezing

cloudy

THE SEASONS

A   Practise with the teacher.

Spring	Summer	Fall (autumn)	Winter
March	June	September	December
April	July	October	January
May	August	November	February

1. It's spring.
2. It's summer.
3. It's fall/autumn.
4. It's winter.

a thermometer

spring

summer

fall/autumn

winter

B   Read the sentences. Choose the answers.

1. March is in spring.   Yes, it is.   No, it isn't.

2. Summer is hot.   Yes, it is.   No, it isn't.

3. April and May are in summer.   Yes, they are.   No, they aren't.

4. February is snowy.   Yes, it is.   No, it isn't.

5. December is in winter.   Yes, it is.   No, it isn't.

6. May is warm.   Yes, it is.   No, it isn't.

7. June and July are in summer.   Yes, they are.   No, they aren't.

8. October is cool.   Yes, it is.   No, it isn't.

C   Write the word that is different.

1. April   January   cool   March

2. hot   cold   cool   spring

3. fall   winter   sunny   summer

4. rainy   December   snowy   sunny

CANADIAN CAPSULES   Many parts of Canada are very cold in the winter, and very hot in the summer.

temperature   leaves   grass   trees   water

CLOTHING

A   Look at the pictures. Practise with the teacher.

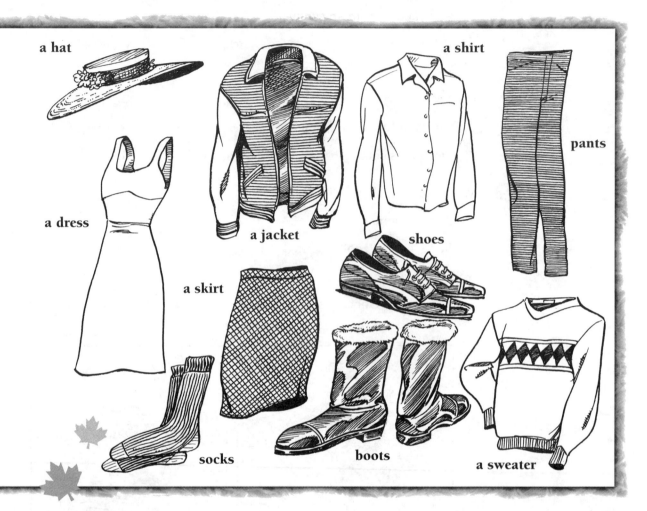

a hat

a dress

a jacket

a shirt

pants

a skirt

shoes

socks

boots

a sweater

CANADIAN CAPSULES   Victoria and Vancouver, BC, are not too hot in the summer and they are not too cold in the winter. There isn't much snow in the winter in Victoria and Vancouver.

a hat

a dress

a shirt

pants

socks

B   What are they wearing? Look at the pictures. Copy the chart. Complete the chart.

	Lili	Jun	Mona	Michel
a hat				
a jacket or coat				
shoes	✔			
boots				
a dress	✔			
a sweater				
pants				
socks				

shoes   a skirt   a jacket   boots   a sweater

BUYING CLOTHES

LISTENING ACTIVITY 11

A   Look at the pictures. Answer the questions.

1. How much is the sweater?
2. How much are the shoes?
3. How much are the socks?
4. How much is the jacket?

5. How much are the boots?
6. How much is the dress?
7. How much is the hat?
8. How much are the pants?

a coat

a scarf

gloves

mitts

a T-shirt

B   Practise with the teacher.

Conversation 1

Clerk: Can I help you?

Michel: Yes. How much is this sweater?

Clerk: It's $35.

Michel: Thank you.

Clerk: You're welcome.

Conversation 2

Clerk: Can I help you?

Olga: Yes. How much is this sweater?

Clerk: It's $45.

Olga: That's too much.

Clerk: This sweater is only $30.

Olga: That's fine. I'll take it.

C   Listen and write the words. Use the worksheet.

Conversation 1

Clerk: Can I help you?

Ana: Yes. How much is this jacket?

Clerk: It's _____.

Ana: Oh, that's too much. How _____ is this one?

Clerk: It's _____.

Ana: OK. I'll take it.

jeans

hot

cold

tired

thirsty

Conversation 2

Clerk: Can I help you?

Carlos: Yes. _____ much is this hat?

Clerk: It's _____.

Carlos: Oh, that's too much. How _____ is this one?

Clerk: It's _____.

Carlos: OK. I'll take it.

D Practise the conversations with a partner.

E Work with a partner. Write a conversation about buying clothes.

HOW DO YOU FEEL?

A Look at the pictures. Practise with the teacher.

She's hot.

She's tired.

We're happy.

He's cold.

He's sad.

She's thirsty.

sad

happy

short sleeves

long sleeves

expensive

B Look at the pictures. Match the pictures to the sentences on page 152.

> The dress is too big.   **c**

1. His pants are too short.
2. The shoes are too small.
3. The sweater is too expensive.
4. This sweater is too warm.
5. She is tired.

6. We're hot and thirsty.
7. This hat is new.
8. These socks are old.
9. They are cold.
10. She's is sad.

TRAVEL

A   Look at the suitcases. Read the stories on page 153. Write the names for the suitcases.

a suitcase

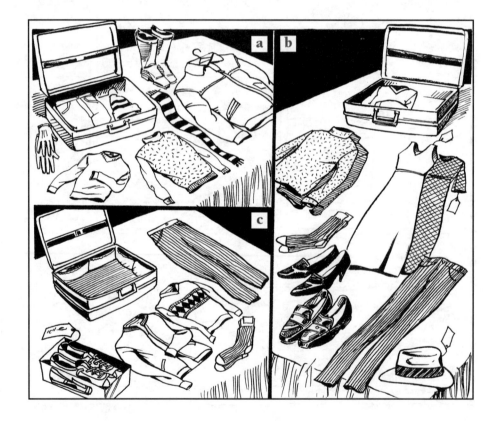

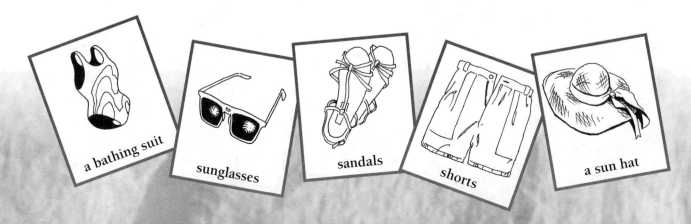

a bathing suit

sunglasses

sandals

shorts

a sun hat

1. It is summer. Max and Olga are in Italy. They have a big suitcase. They have pants and sweaters. They have socks and shoes. Olga has two new dresses. Max has a new hat.

2. It is March. Lili is in Alaska. It is very cold. She has a jacket and two sweaters. She has a warm hat. She has pants and she has warm boots.

3. It is December. Mona is in Florida with her family. It is sunny, but it is cool. She has one sweater, and pants. She has a jacket too. She has socks and new shoes.

B   Complete the postcards.

is

you

I

are

Dear Kate,

How _____ you?
How _____ the
weather in Spain? Is the
summer hot or cold? Are
_____ happy there?
It is very cold here, but
_____ am happy.

Write soon,
Lili

Dear Jun,

How are you? We're fine. How is
the _____ in New York?
Is it _____? How is your
brother? It's _____ and
warm here, in Italy. We are very
_____.

Write soon,
Max and Olga

hot

weather

happy

sunny

a blouse   a suit   a tie   a pocket   a belt

Dear Michel,

How are you? I am in Florida.
It is a little _____, but it
is sunny. I have a warm
_____. How are you? Is
it cold and _____? Are
you _____?

Write soon,
Mona

sweater

cool

tired

snowy

WORD GAME

Find these words. Circle the words. Use the worksheet.

A   Cold weather:

cold   hat   snowy   winter   sweater   jacket   boots

```
b  a  e  t  w  i  n  t  e  r  c  o
b  e  s  w  e  a  t  e  r  f  y  l
k  e  g  s  t  j  a  c  k  e  t  y
s  e  c  e  v  c  b  o  o  t  s  z
x  z  c  o  l  d  y  q  w  p  b  c
r  f  s  n  o  w  y  i  d  y  t  c
i  o  p  s  g  h  a  t  w  t  h  e
```

sneakers

pyjamas

a nightgown

slippers

pantyhose

B   Hot weather:

pants   shoes   socks   sunny   warm   weather

```
w e a t h e r x t b d g
e t y w s h o e s c b n
s i e b c w a r m i h e
p i y b c s u n n y e t
s o c k s e i b n t q t
e t i p a n t s e m c n
```

an umbrella   a raincoat   rainboots   a tuque   a snowsuit

WORD REVIEW

Write the words for the pictures.

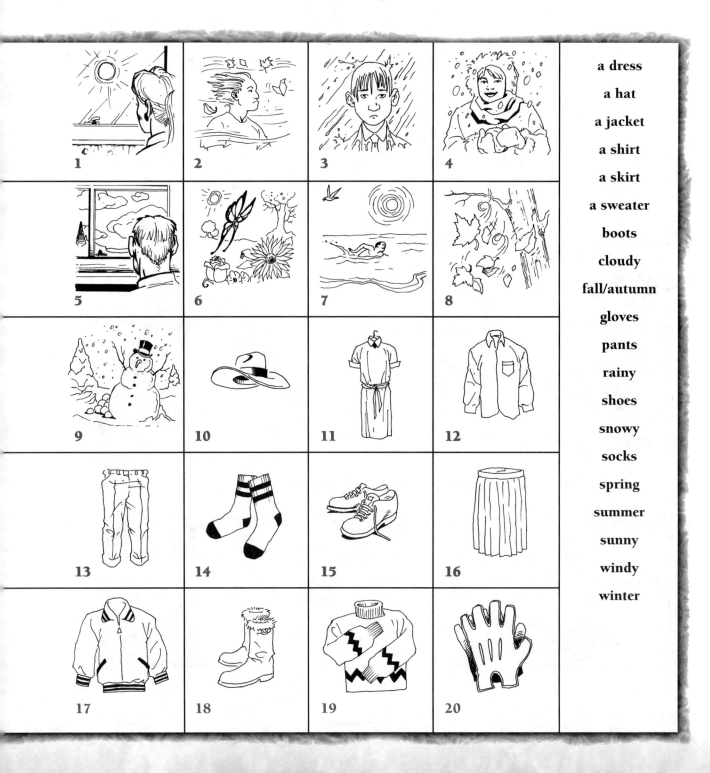

a dress

a hat

a jacket

a shirt

a skirt

a sweater

boots

cloudy

fall/autumn

gloves

pants

rainy

shoes

snowy

socks

spring

summer

sunny

windy

winter

Englisch ist einfach

ben englizce oranmak stiurum

私は英語が好きです。

أنا أحب هذا الكتاب

Vaya suka buku ini

Bu Kitapi cok seudim

我會説英文

See you in Canadian Concepts 2!

Delam mikhad englisi yad begiram

नमस्ते फिर मिलेंगे

Mi piace molto questo libro

WITHDRAWN FROM COLLECTION

Tôi thích quyển sách này

Inglès é fácil de aprender.

Je parle anglais

안녕

私はこの本が大好きです。

Μιλαω Εγγλινικά

ME GUSTA HABLAR INGLES

Μοι αρέσει αυτό το βιβλίο